2nd edition

Python for finance and algorithmic trading

Lucas INGLESE

A question to ask the author? Section 1.3 "Join the community"

Table of contents

Why should you read this book?

The financial sector is undergoing significant restructuring. Traders and portfolio managers are increasingly becoming financial data scientists. Banks, hedge funds, and fintech are automating their investments by integrating machine learning and deep learning algorithms into their decision-making process. **This book presents the benefits of portfolio management, statistics, and machine learning applied to live trading with MetaTrader 5.**

Part 1 is dedicated to **portfolio management, risk management, and back testing.** These chapters will allow us to understand how to combine strategies and which metrics to look at to understand the strategy robustness.

Part 2 discusses **statistical predictive models**. We will discuss the statistical arbitrage and autoregressive moving average (ARMA) model and introduce the classification algorithms through logistic regression.

Part 3 gives us an understanding of **Machine Learning and Deep Learning predictive models**. We will see these algorithms using trading strategies example: Support Vector Machines (SVM), decision tree, random forest, ensemble methods, Artificial Neural Network (ANN), Recurrent Neural Network (RNN), Recurrent Convolutional Neural Network (RCNN)

The book ends with a **concrete project from A to Z:** Importing data from your broker, creating a portfolio of trading strategies, deployment in live trading, or using a screener.

Who am I?

I am Lucas, an independent quantitative trader specializing in Machine learning and data science and the founder of Quantreo, an algorithmic trading E-learning website (www.quantreo.com).

I graduated in mathematics and economics from the University of Strasbourg (France). I already help more than 56.000 students through my online courses and YouTube channel dedicated to algorithmic trading.

I have a quantitative trading approach, combining predictive models, financial theory, and stochastic calculus.

To show you some realistic results, you can see the profit of my last portfolio of strategies in live trading: **2.5% of return** for a **0.6% drawdown** without leverage in 1 month and a half.

Figure 1: My last live trading signal on BullTrading

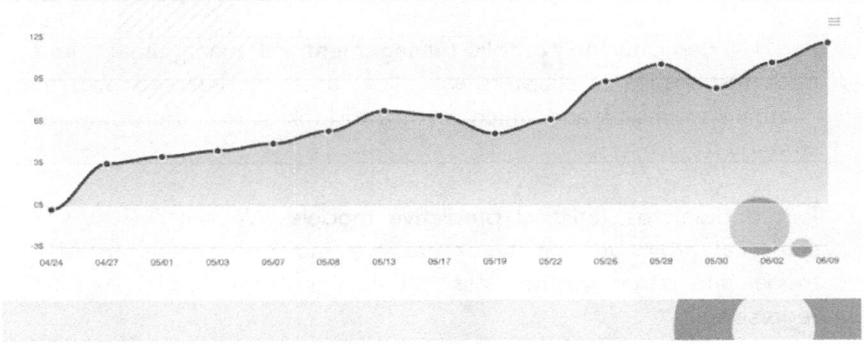

Your Statistics

Current capital	Winning Trades	Losing trades	Ratio of winning trades (%)	Losses	Profits	Fees	Your net profits*
172.45 $	50	43	53.76 %	-20.73 $	+34.59 $	-2.38 $	11.48 $

You can see one of my last signals on BullTrading (bulltrading.be), a copy trader platform. This strategy is based on machine learning and quantitative analysis (the same as in the book).

Chapter 1: Read me

1.1. Find the code

All the resources in the book are available on the GitHub repository (https://github.com/Quantreo/2nd-edition-BOOK-AMAZON-Python-for-Finance-and-Algorithmic-Trading). If there is an issue with this link or something else related to the code, contact us using the contact page www.quantreo.com.

Before reading this book, you should download Jupyter Notebook using Anaconda Navigator (https://www.anaconda.com). In Chapter 01, you can find a notebook that installs all the necessary libraries for the book. All the additional readings can be found on the README.md file on the repository Github.

1.2. Conventions used in this book

This box gives precision, suggestions, or tips usually used in finance, trading, or data sciences.

This box gives precision, suggestions, or tips about the code.

This box gives precision, suggestions, or tips from the author's experience.

Italic content: explain the figures

1.3. Join our community

Follow us on social media to obtain the latest algorithmic trading information, tips, and ready-to-use strategies. Moreover, join the discord forum of the community to ask any questions about the book to read it easily!

Linktree QRCODE

Chapter 2: Prerequisites

This chapter discusses the necessary prerequisites to understand this book thoroughly. First, we will discuss some math, statistics, algebra, and optimization basics. Then, the leading financial theories and the Python basics are mandatory to implement our trading strategies.

2.1. Mathematical prerequisites

This section aims to detail many mathematical terms and concepts necessary for the book's whole comprehension. However, it is not complete math for the finance course. We will cover some introductory algebra, statistics, and optimization.

2.1.1. Algebra

Algebra is a significant field to know when we work in finance. Indeed, we will work with matrices all the time because it is the heart of algebra. Thus, it is required to understand the basics about them.

There are many theories about matrices in math, more complex than others, but for us, it will be straightforward: a matrix will be a set of data. Let us see an example of a matrix A with shape (n,m), where m is the number of columns and n is the number of rows in the matrix.

$$A = \begin{pmatrix} 1 & 0.7 \\ -1 & -3 \\ 0.6 & 0.1 \end{pmatrix}$$

We can imagine that matrix A with a shape of (3,2) will give us the daily return of some assets. Usually, the rows will be the days, and the columns represent the assets. Thus, the matrix has two assets and three daily returns for each.

There are many essential operations that we can apply to a matrix. Let us see some of them:

- **Addition**: we need matrices with the same shape to add them. Then, we must add matrix A's coefficients to matrix B's coefficients, one by one. Let us take an example to explain.

$$\begin{pmatrix} 1 & 1 \\ 2 & 3 \end{pmatrix} + \begin{pmatrix} 1 & 1 \\ 1 & 1 \end{pmatrix} = \begin{pmatrix} 1+1 & 1+1 \\ 2+1 & 3+1 \end{pmatrix}$$

- **Subtraction**: We need matrices with the same shape to add them. Then, we must subtract the coefficients of matrix A from the coefficients of matrix B, one by one. Let us take an example to explain.

$$\begin{pmatrix} 1 & 1 \\ 2 & 3 \end{pmatrix} - \begin{pmatrix} 1 & 1 \\ 1 & 1 \end{pmatrix} = \begin{pmatrix} 1-1 & 1-1 \\ 2-1 & 3-1 \end{pmatrix}$$

- **Scalar multiplication**: We multiply each coefficient by the scalar (just a number). Let us take an example to explain.

$$3 * \begin{pmatrix} 1 & 1 \\ 2 & 3 \end{pmatrix} = \begin{pmatrix} 3*1 & 3*1 \\ 3*2 & 3*3 \end{pmatrix}$$

The three previous operations are the basic operations between matrices but exist more complex operations like inverse, comatrix, and transpose. Thankfully, we only need to know the transpose matrix for the rest of this book. Suppose each matrix coefficient is noted $a_{i,j}$ where i is the row number and j the column number of the coefficient. All matrix coefficients A $a_{i,j}$ become $a_{j,i}$ in the transpose matrix called A^t. Let's take an example to explain it.

$$\begin{pmatrix} 1 & 4 \\ 2 & 5 \\ 3 & 6 \end{pmatrix}^t = \begin{pmatrix} 1 & 2 & 3 \\ 4 & 5 & 6 \end{pmatrix}$$

2.1.2. Statistics

Statistics are mandatory when we work in quantitative finance. From calculating the returns to the computation of probabilities, we will see the necessary skills to work on a financial project with peace of mind. First, we will see some statistical metrics, but do not worry if you do not understand them 100% because we will discuss them later in the book! To compute an example of each metric, we will work with these vectors (vectors are matrices with a shape (1,n)) $v = (1,2,3)$ and $u = (0,1,3)$.

- **Mean**: It is the most detailed statistic. It is the sum of all values divided by the number of values.

$$\bar{v} = \frac{1}{N}\sum_{i=1}^{N} v_i = \frac{1}{3} * (1 + 2 + 3) = 2$$

- **Variance**: The variance is a measure of the dispersion of values in a sample. This metric allows an understanding of how much the values are dispersed around the mean.

$$Var = \frac{1}{N}\sum_{i=1}^{N}(v_i - \bar{v})^2 = \frac{1}{3} * ((-1)^2 + 0^2 + 1^2 = \frac{2}{3} = 0.67$$

- **Standard deviation**: The variance is a measure of the dispersion of values in a sample. This metric also allows us to understand the values' dispersion around the mean. It is the squared root of the variance. In finance, it allows us to compute the volatility of an asset.

$$\sigma = \sqrt{Var} = \sqrt{\frac{2}{3}}$$

- **Cumulative sum**: This metric returns a vector, not only a float. A cumulative sum is a sequence of partial sums of a given sequence.

$$v_j = \sum_{i=1}^{j} v_i = (1, 1 + 2, 1 + 2 + 3) = (1,3,6)$$

- **Cumulative product**: This metric returns a vector, not only a float. It does the product of all the values before for each coefficient.

$$v_j = \prod_{i=1}^{j} v_i = (1, 1 * 2, 1 * 2 * 3) = (1,2,6)$$

- **Mean squared error (MSE):** This metric is used to compute the loss of an algorithm which allows us to train it (but we will talk more about it later). To penalize the significant error, it will compute all the differences between predictions and actual values. We need two vectors or matrices with the same shapes.

$$MSE = \sum_{i=1}^{N} (v_i - u_i)^2 = 1^2 + 1^2 + 0^2 = 2$$

- **Mean absolute error (MAE):** This metric is also used to compute the loss of an algorithm. It will compute all the differences between predictions and take the absolute value of the subtraction. We need two vectors or matrices with the same shapes.

$$MAE = \sum_{i=1}^{N} |v_i - u_i| = 1 + 1 + 0 = 2$$

Where |-x| = |x| = x. It means that the absolute value takes only the values not the sign.

Now, let us discuss statistic tests. There are many, but we will see only one in this book, which is essential to understand: the augmented Dick and Fuller test. However, first, let us explain how a statistic test generally works. Usually, there are two hypotheses: H0 and H1. The objective of the test is to test the H0 hypothesis.

It is a vast and exciting field that can be covered in an entire book. So, we will try to make it simple quickly. When we perform a statistical test, we will have only two possibilities: we reject H0, or we cannot reject H0. To find the situation we are in, we will use the p-value (a value between 0 and 1). The following rules can be applied to every hypothesis test; if we take an error threshold **s** and the p-value of a test which is called p, we have these two possibilities:

- **p > s:** we can't reject H0
- **p < s:** we can reject H0

Finally, we need to discuss probability laws. They are essential in finance because they allow us to understand how the observations are distributed. The most used law in finance is the normal law. Thus, we will illustrate the following notion taking it. There are two essential functions in a probability law:

- **Cumulative distribution function or repartition function (CDF):** This function returns the probability that the random variable X is below the value x. The CDF takes in all absolute values and returns a value between 0 and 1 because it is a probability. Let us formalize this a little bit.

$$F_X(x): \mathbb{R} \to [0,1]$$

$$F_X(x) = P(X < x)$$

- **Probability density function (PDF):** This function allows us to understand the distributions of observations. Let us see inf figure 2.1 the difference between CDF and PDF.

Figure 2.1: CDF and PDF for the normal law

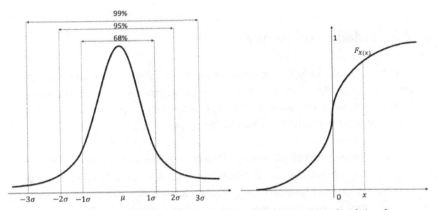

We can see the CDF to the right and the PDF to the left of the figure. However, the percentage between the standard deviation interval is only available with a normal law, not for the others.

2.1.3. Optimization

When we talk about portfolio management, it always implies talking about optimization. The optimization methods allow us to minimize or maximize a function under constraints. For example, in portfolio management, we maximize the portfolio's utility under constraints that the portfolio's weight must equal 100%. Let us take an example of an optimization problem explaining each part.

$$\max_{\sum w_i = 100\%} U(w)$$

The function to maximize is $U(w)$, and we want to maximize it. However, we have a constraint $\sum w_i = 100\%$ which meaning we want to invest all our capital. The vector of the weights w is the variable that allows us to optimize the function.

2.2. Prerequisites in finance

This section will explain some mandatory theories to know before creating some algorithmic trading strategies: market efficiency, basics of trading, and portfolio management theory.

2.2.1. Market efficiency

The theory of market efficiency implies that we cannot predict the stock behavior because it is a random walk. However, it is the theory. In practice, it is possible to predict stock behavior. Let us see the different levels of efficiency to explain that.

- **Weak market efficiency**: This part implies that it is impossible to predict the stock price using past prices. Thus, the stock price is a random walk. However, we can predict the future stock price using machine learning techniques. This book will only use quantitative predictive models to prove that weak efficiency is not always respected.

- **Semi-strong market efficiency**: This part implies that all the information is always considered in the stock's prices. It means that we cannot make a profit using the news. Indeed, the market should already consider the news before it comes using the previsions of the investors. However, it is possible to prove that the semi-strong efficiency market is not always respected using Natural Language Processing (NLP). For example, using machine learning algorithms, we can use tweets, news, and TV to find opportunities.

- **Strong market efficiency:** This part implies that all the information is available to anybody. However, it is incorrect because the firm's CEO can access some information that private investors do not have. It can be used to make a profit on the market. Thus, this proves that the strong efficiency market is not always respected. However, we cannot use algorithms to predict it.

2.2.2. Basics of trading

When we talk about trading in this book, we speak only about speculative trading. The goal is to make profit using **CFD (Contract for Differences).**

A Contract for Differences (CFD) is a derivative that follows the same variation as its underlying. The advantage of the CFD is that we can bet on the decrease of the stock. It is called **shorting** an asset (we will discuss that later).

When we buy a CFD, we will pay some fees. These fees are either commission or spread. The **spread** is the difference between the bid price and the asking price. Moreover, the **commissions** are a fixed amount that we will pay the broker **to enter positions and exit.**

The last notion that we need to know is **leverage**. A financial tool available when we open an account with the broker allows, we to multiply the strategy's returns. Thus, it is good when we earn money and wrong when we lose it. Leverage is a powerful tool that can be a destructor of our capital in the wrong hands (reminder: with great power comes great responsibility)
Usually, leverage is taken by the account and not by each trade. As we said earlier, leverage increases the risk of losing money. However, it allows people with little capital to invest in the market. So, in practice, it is strongly recommended to work on accounts with capital coverage, which means that the broker closes our positions before we run out of capital so that we do not get into debt with the broker, even though

during extremely volatile movements, we may owe the broker money if he could not close the positions in time.

There is another variable that we need to consider: the **swap**. It is an interest paid to the broker to keep the position open the night. As the swap is a difference in interest rates, it can be negative or positive.

When we have opened trades, we can set a **Stop Loss** (SL) or a **Take Profit** (TP). The stop loss is a threshold that is the associate's price to the worst loss that we want to accept. It means that if we do not want to lose more than 1% of our capital, we set our stop loss at the asset price, which makes we lose only 1% of the capital. For example, we have 100$ of capital, and we want to limit the loss on this position to 1%. If we are in an extended position, we will set the stop loss at 99$. If the price goes below 99$, the position is closed automatically. It allows us to limit the risk of the investment. The take profit is the same thing but with the inverse reflection. We will close the position when we earn the desired amount.

2.2.3. Basics of portfolio management

The goal of portfolio management is to invest using technic to reduce the portfolio's risk (diversification). The foundation of portfolio management was put in place by M.Markovitz (1952). The mean-variance portfolio theory was the basis of the portfolio management technique. Indeed, the first theory focuses more on statistics than the other parameters. It will be the foundation of our static portfolio analysis.

2.3. Prerequisites in Python

In this part, we will discuss the main functions of the libraries for data science, math, and finance that we will use.

2.3.1. Libraries for data sciences

Numpy

np.array(obj)	create an array
np.zeros([n,m])	create a matrix of size (n,m)
np.ones([n,m])	create a matrix full of one
np.mean(array, axis=)	return the mean of the array
np.std(array, axis=)	return the standard deviation of the array
np.var(array, axis=)	return the variance of the array
np.sum(array,axis=)	return the sum of the array
np.cumprod(array, axis=)	return the cumulative product of the array
np.where(condition, value_true, value_false)	apply condition to a numpy array
np.concatenate([arr,...],axis=)	concatenate some arrays

Pandas

pd.DataFrame(obj, index=[], columns=[])	create a dataframe
df.columns = [col,...,col]	change the columns of a dataframe
pd.Series(obj, index=[])	create a series

Matplotlib

plt.figure()	modify the figure
plt.plot(x,y)	plot a line
plt.fill_between(x,y,condition)	plot an area
plt.title("title")	give a title
plt.xlabel("title")	give x label
plt.ylabel ("title")	give y label
plt.legend([col,...,col])	name the legend
plt.xlim([a,b])	Resize the limit
plt.show()	show a figure

21

2.3.2. Libraries for finance

Yfinance

yf.download(ticker, start=, end=)	download stock price

Datetime

datetime.now()	give the date in datetime format
datetime.now().strftime(%Y-%m-%d)	datetime to string
datetime.now().week()	Find weekday

Time

time.sleep(n)	Put the computer in a break of n seconds

2.3.3. Libraries for mathematics

Scipy

scipy.optimize.minimize(criterion, x, args=())	Minimize a function

StatsModels

statsmodels.tsa.stattools.adfuller(arr)	Compute adfuller test
statsmodels.api.stat.OLS(x,y).fit()	Train model
model.resid()	Give the residuals
statsmodels.tsa.arima_model.ARIMA(arr)	Compute ARIMA model
statsmodels.graphics.tsaplots.plot_acf(arr)	Plot the acf

statsmodels.graphics.tsaplots.plot_pcaf(arr)	Plot the pacf

Part 1: Portfolio management, risk management and backtesting

In this part, we will discuss static portfolio optimization methods, such as mean-variance optimization and Sharpe ratio optimization. We will also see some dynamic portfolio optimization, such as momentum criteria. Once we have created some portfolios, we will analyze the risk of these portfolios and backtest them.

Summary:

Chapter 3: Static portfolio optimization

Chapter 4: Dynamic portfolio optimization

Chapter 5: Risk management and backtesting

Chapter 6: Advanced backtest methods

Chapter 3: Static Portfolio management

This chapter will discuss static portfolio optimization methods. First, we will see the intuition behind portfolio optimization and why they are so valuable for portfolio management. Then, we will look at the traditional portfolio optimization method like the mean-variance criterion or mean-variance skewness kurtosis criterion. Moreover, we will study how to do our criterion for portfolio optimization.

3.1. Explanation behind portfolio optimization method

This section will explain why portfolio optimization is so valuable in finance. First, we will see the difference between systemic and specific risks. Then, we highlight the advantages of diversification.

3.1.1. Systemic risk and specific risk

When we talk about the risk of an asset, we think about asset volatility. In contrast, we can decompose the risk of an asset in two ways: the systemic risk and the specific risk.

Asset-specific risk is the risk associated with an asset that does not depend on market conditions. For example, an issue in a factory of Tesla can reduce the price of the Tesla stock but only the Tesla stock because there are no reasons that this issue affects the Netflix stock price, for example.

The systemic risk is a macroeconomic risk on all the economy's assets. For example, suppose there is a significant recession caused by geopolitical instability. In that case, all stock prices will decrease because people do not want to consume because of the uncertainty of the future. It is a systemic risk because it affects all the economy's assets.

The big difference between specific and systemic risk is that the systemic risk does not depend on the firm's actions. Thus, the objective of the portfolio optimization methods is to reduce the specific risk in the portfolio. To do that, we use diversification.

 This book only sees how to reduce the specific risk, but it is possible to reduce the systemic risk using derivatives.

3.1.2. Diversification

Diversification is the core process of portfolio management. It allows us to reduce the specific risk of the portfolio, as explained above. The strategy aims to increase the number of assets in the portfolio to make the specific risk of each asset insignificant. The explanation is shown in figure 3.1.

Figure 3.1: Risk of portfolio

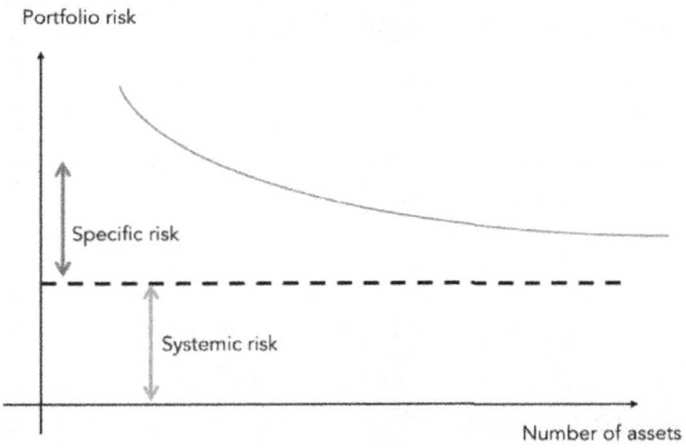

Portfolio risk

Specific risk

Systemic risk

Number of assets

In this figure, we see the decomposition of the risk between the specific risk and systemic risk. The more the number of asset increases, the more we are closer to the systemic portfolio risk.

The figure shows that the increase in the number of assets allows us to reduce the portfolio's risk to the portfolio's systemic risk because each asset's specific risk decreases with the number of assets. So, the figure highlights the power of diversification to decrease the risk of a portfolio.

Diversification decreases the specific risk to a theoretical level of 0, but in practice, the cost of the transaction or tax forces to limit the diversification a little and find a reasonable allocation considering the cost of the transaction.

3.2. The traditional portfolio optimization methods

In this section, we will learn the traditional portfolio optimization methods. This book will not focus on the theory of the portfolio utility function but only on this calculation and its advantages[1]. Next, we will use a derivative of the portfolio utility function to create advanced diversification criteria.

3.2.1. Portfolio utility function

We will explain some exciting results about the portfolio utility function and the process we will follow in the following parts. The portfolio utility function is the main point in portfolio management theory. Indeed, with this function, we can quantify the satisfaction given by the portfolio. Naturally, we will use this function to maximize the investor's utility.

The utility function is tough to compute in its original form. Thus, to avoid this issue, we will use the Taylor approximation of this function to find the mean-variance and the mean-variance skewness kurtosis criterion.

The equation $U_{MV}(w)$ is the mean-variance criterion, and the $U_{SK}(w)$ is the mean-variance-skewness-kurtosis criterion. In the following

---

[1] **Additional lecture**: Markowitz's "Portfolio Selection ": A Fifty-Year Retrospective

equation, μ is the mean of the portfolio's returns, σ the portfolio's volatility, s the skewness of the portfolio, and k the kurtosis of the portfolio. Moreover, λ is the level of risk aversion (we set it at 3 because it is a usual risk aversion), $\overline{w}$ the risk-free wealth (we set 1.0025), and w the wealth of the portfolio.

$$U_{MV}(w) = \frac{\overline{w}^{1-\lambda}}{1+\lambda} + \overline{w}^{-\lambda}w\mu - \frac{\lambda}{2}\overline{w}^{-1-\lambda}w^2\sigma^2$$

$$U_{SK}(w) = U_{MV}(w) + \frac{\lambda(\lambda+1)}{6}\overline{w}^{-2-\lambda}w^3s - \frac{\lambda(\lambda+1)(\lambda+2)}{24}\overline{w}^{-3-\lambda}w^4k$$

Don't worry we will show you how to compute it in the next section!

3.2.2. Mean-variance criterion

In this subsection, we will implement a mean-variance optimization[2]. It is necessary to download a database with some assets' adjusted close stock prices. To do the portfolio optimization, we will use these assets: Facebook, Netflix, and Tesla. For the importation, we will use the library *yfinance*, which allows us to import data very quickly. Moreover, we transform the data into daily variation to put all assets on the same scale.

Code 3.1: Importation of data

```
# Importation of data
list_tickers = ["FB", "NFLX", "TSLA"] 1
database = yf.download(list_tickers) 2


# Take only the adjusted stock price
database = database["Adj Close"] 3


# Drop missing values
data = database.dropna().pct_change(1).dropna() 4
```

1   Create a list of tickers using the Yahoo notation.

---

[2] **Additional lecture:** *Portfolio management: mean-variance analysis in the US asset market.*

2   Use the *download()* function of *yfinance* to import the dataset.

3   Select only the adjusted close prices.

4   Create returns and remove missing values.

Figure 3.2: Extract from the database

Date	05-21	05-22	05-23	05-24	05-25	05-29
Facebook	-0.110	-0.089	0.032	0.032	-0.34	-0.096
Netflix	0.025	-0.056	0.062	-0.023	-0.001	-0.011
Tesla	0.044	0.071	0.007	-0.024	-0.016	0.063

Extract from the database from code 3.1, which imports the data of Facebook (FB), Netflix (NFLX), and Tesla (TSLA) from 2012 to 2021.

Now, we need to define the function *MV_criterion* to calculate the utility of the function and find the best distribution among the three assets. To do it, we will compute the equation in part 3.2.1 ($U_{MV}(w)$).

Code 3.2: mean-variance criterion function

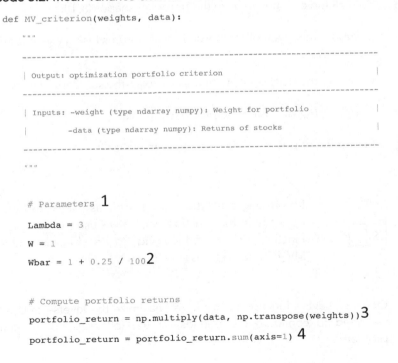

```
def MV_criterion(weights, data):
    """

    ------------------------------------------------------------

    | Output: optimization portfolio criterion                 |

    ------------------------------------------------------------

    | Inputs: -weight (type ndarray numpy): Weight for portfolio |

    |         -data (type ndarray numpy): Returns of stocks      |

    ------------------------------------------------------------

    """


    # Parameters 1

    Lambda = 3

    W = 1

    Wbar = 1 + 0.25 / 100 2


    # Compute portfolio returns

    portfolio_return = np.multiply(data, np.transpose(weights)) 3

    portfolio_return = portfolio_return.sum(axis=1) 4
```

29

```
# Compute mean and volatility of the portfolio
mean = np.mean(portfolio_return, axis=0) 5
std = np.std(portfolio_return, axis=0) 6


# Compute the criterion
criterion = Wbar ** (1 - Lambda) / (1 + Lambda) + Wbar ** (-Lambda)
\ * W * mean - Lambda / 2 * Wbar ** (-1 - Lambda) * W ** 2 *\ std
** 2 7


criterion = -criterion 8
return criterion
```

1   Set the parameters of the model above.

2   The risk-free wealth is 1 + the risk-free rate (0.25%).

3   Multiply the columns by their coefficient to keep a matrix with shape (n,m).

4   Sum all the columns to have the portfolio (shape=(n,1)).

5   Compute the mean of the portfolio daily returns (using axis=0 to do on the rows).

6   Compute the daily volatility of the portfolio (the standard deviation).

7   Compute $U_{MV}(w)$ using the previous formula.

8   Return the opposite of the criterion to minimize it.

Maximizing a function is the same as minimizing the opposite of this function. So, we will use the minimize function in the following code because the MV_criterion returns us $-U_{MV}(w)$.

Once we have a function to minimize (maximize the inverse of U(w)), we need to configure the bounds for the following optimization problem.

$$\max_{\Sigma \alpha_i=1} U_{MV}(w)$$

It means we will maximize the utility under the constraints to use all the capital because the sum of α_i must equal 100%. Therefore, we need to use all our capital. Thus, the bounds for each asset are (0,1).

We also need to set a weight for the start of the optimization. Furthermore, we will only perform the optimization on the train set (70% of the data) and analyze the test set's performance (30% of the data).

Code 3.3: Implementation of the portfolio optimization problem

```
split = int(0.7 * len(data)) 1

train_set = data.iloc[:split, :]

test_set = data.iloc[split:, :]


# Find the number of assets
n = data.shape[1] 2


# Initialization weight value
x0 = np.ones(n) 3


# Optimization constraints problem
cons = ({'type': 'eq', 'fun': lambda x: sum(abs(x)) - 1}) 4


# Set the bounds
Bounds = [(0, 1) for i in range(0, n)] 5


# Optimization problem solving
res_MV = minimize(MV_criterion, x0, method="SLSQP",
                  args=(train_set), bounds=Bounds,
                  constraints=cons, options={'disp': True}) 6


# Result
X_MV = res_MV.x 7
```

1   The variable split is an integer representing the value at 70% of the data. It is a tip to select the train and test sets.

2   n is the number of assets, so we use the command *.shape[1]* to have the number of columns which is the number of assets.

3   Initialize the value of the weight vector. It is a vector full of one with a shape (n,).

4   Define the constraints of the optimization. Here, we want the investor to use all its capital. Thus, we wish that the sum of the weight equal 100%. (There is absolute value if we wish to short also).

5   Define the bound of the optimization. We define the bounds from 0 to 1 because we want a long-only strategy. If we create a long-short strategy, *bounds* will be (-1,1).

6   Minimize the opposite of the $U_{MV}(w)$ using the *minimize* function of *scipy*.

7   Extract the optimal weight for our portfolio.

With the previous code, we have found the best allocation for this asset and, the vector of the weights is available in figure 3.3.

Figure 3.3: Weights allocation of the portfolio using MV criterion

Asset	Facebook	Netflix	Tesla
Weight	33.35%	33.35%	33.30%

As we can see, the optimization with the MV criterion takes the Facebook stock for 33.35%, the Netflix stock for 33.35%, and the Tesla stock for 33.30%.

Now, we have the weights of each asset in our portfolio. So, we need to display the returns of the portfolio on the test set to see if the portfolio optimization is good or not. Even if the cumulative returns of the portfolio cannot say alone if it is a good optimization or not, it is a good indication.

Code 3.4: Testing performance on test set

```
# Compute the cumulative return of the portfolio (CM)
portfolio_return_MV = np.multiply(test_set,np.transpose(X_MV))    1
portfolio_return_MV = portfolio_return_MV.sum(axis=1) 2


# Plot the CM
plt.figure(figsize=(15,8)) 3
plt.plot(np.cumsum(portfolio_return_MV)*100,
 color="#035593", linewidth=3) 4
plt.ylabel("Cumulative return %", size=15, fontweight="bold") 5
plt.xticks(size=15,fontweight="bold")
plt.yticks(size=15,fontweight="bold")
plt.title("Cumulative   return   of   the   mean   variance   potfolio",
size=20)
plt.axhline(0, color="r",linewidth=3) 6
plt.show() 7
```

1   We have multiple columns by his coefficient. Thus, we always have a shape (n,m) matrix.

2   We do the sum of each column to have the portfolio return.

3   We change the size of the figure to have a better visualization.

4   Print the cumulative sum of the portfolio and put it in percentages.

5   Put a name and increase the size of the y-labels.

6   Put a horizontal line at 0 to highlight this threshold.

7   We show the graph using *plt.show()*.

In figure 3.4, we can see the plot of the cumulative return on the test set. It is good to see the portfolio's return, but only in the next chapter will we learn how to complete risk analysis and backtest.

Indeed, we will see many metrics such as Sharpe and Sortino ratios, drawdown, and the CPAM metrics to only give them as an example.

Figure 3.4: Cumulative return of the portfolio on the test set

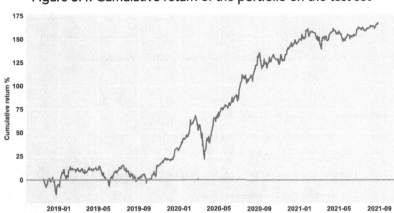

As we can see, the cumulative return of the portfolio is stagnant in the first year. However, after this period, the portfolio's return has considerable growth.

3.2.3. Mean-variance-skewness-kurtosis criterion

In the last subsection, we have seen the mean-variance criterion. In this subsection, we will see an extension of the mean-variance criterion: the mean-variance-skewness-kurtosis criterion[3] (SK criterion). We are going to take precisely the same data to compare the optimizations. Here, we will use the $U_{SK}(w)$ and not $U_{MV}(w)$ as a criterion. So, we will see the difference in the weight with different criteria.

Code 3.6: SK criterion Implementation

```
def SK_criterion(weights, data):
    """

    ------------------------------------------------------------------------

    | Output: optimization portfolio criterion                             |

    ------------------------------------------------------------------------

    | Inputs: -weight (type ndarray numpy): Weight for portfolio           |
    |         -data (type ndarray numpy): Returns of stocks                |

    ------------------------------------------------------------------------
```

---

[3] **Additional lecture** : *Mean-variance-skewness-kurtosis based portfolio optimization*

```
"""
from scipy.stats import skew, kurtosis

# Parameters 1

Lambda = 3

W = 1

Wbar = 1 + 0.25 / 100


# Compute portfolio returns 2

portfolio_return = np.multiply(data, np.transpose(weights))

portfolio_return = portfolio_return.sum(axis=1)


# Compute mean, volatility, skew, kurtosis of the portfolio

mean = np.mean(portfolio_return, axis=0)

std = np.std(portfolio_return, axis=0)

skewness = skew(portfolio_return, 0) 3

kurt = kurtosis(portfolio_return, 0) 4


# Compute the criterion

criterion = Wbar ** (1 - Lambda) / (1 + Lambda) + Wbar ** (-Lambda) \

    * W * mean - Lambda / 2 * Wbar ** (-1 - Lambda) * W ** 2 * std ** 2 \

    + Lambda * (Lambda + 1) / (6) * Wbar ** (-2 - Lambda) * W ** 3 * skewnes\

    - Lambda * (Lambda + 1) * (Lambda + 2) / (24) * Wbar ** (-3 - Lambda) *\

    W ** 4 * kurt 5


criterion = -criterion 6

return criterion
```

1   Set the parameters of the models (*lambda=3* is a typical risk aversion. The higher the lambda, more you hate the risk).

2   Multiple each asset by its coefficient and do the sum to have the portfolio return.

3   Compute the skewness, which calculates the asymmetry of the probability density function (PDF).

4   Compute the kurtosis, which represents the "tailedness" of the probability density function (PDF).

5   Compute $U_{SK}(w)$.

6   Compute the opposite of the criterion because we will minimize it.

Following the same process as the MV criterion, we will do optimization with the SK criterion.

Code 3.7: Optimization with SK criterion

```
# Find the number of assets
n = data.shape[1]


# Initialization weight value
x0 = np.ones(n)


# Optimization constraints problem
cons = ({'type': 'eq', 'fun': lambda x: sum(abs(x)) - 1})


# Set the bounds
Bounds = [(0, 1) for i in range(0, n)]


# Optimization problem solving
res_SK = minimize(SK_criterion, x0, method="SLSQP",
                  args=(train_set), bounds=Bounds,
                  constraints=cons, options={'disp': True})
# Result for computations
X_SK = res_SK.x
```

Figure 3.5: Weights allocation of the portfolio using SK

Asset	Facebook	Netflix	Tesla
Weight	32.75%	21.06%	46.19%

The optimization with the SK criterion takes the Facebook stock for 32.75%, Netflix stock for 21.06%, and Tesla stock for 46.19%.

The weights of the portfolio are different from the MV optimization. The objective is to plot the MV optimization portfolio return and SK optimization portfolio return to compare the best in this situation (Figure 3.6).

36

Figure 3.6: Cumulative returns of the portfolios on the test set

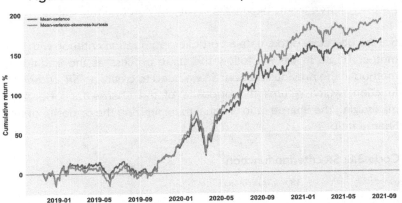

We can see that the two portfolios follow the same trend, but the SK portfolio is a little better than the MV portfolio.

3.3. The modern portfolio optimization methods

In this section, we discuss the modern portfolio optimization method. We will see how to create its criterion using the example of Sharpe and Sortino criteria.

3.3.1. Sharpe criterion

In this subsection, we will speak about the Sharpe criterion. First, we need to define the Sharpe ratio to understand the benefits of this optimization.

The Sharpe ratio is the best known of the financial metrics. Indeed, it is a reference metric in the industry. It allows us to understand the additional benefits for 1% more risk. We can compute the Sharpe ratio with the following formula:

$$Sharpe = \frac{\mu - r_f}{\sigma}$$

37

μ is the mean of the portfolio returns (annualized), σ is the volatility of the portfolio returns (annualized) and r_f is the risk-free asset (we set 0 for the risk-free assets because it is currently around this value).

So, the objective is to create a portfolio optimization criterion with this metric. To do it, we will follow the same process as the traditional method in the previous section. So we need to create an *SR_criterion()* function, which returns the opposite of the Sharpe ratio because maximizing the Sharpe ratio is equal to minimizing the opposite of the Sharpe ratio.

Code 3.8: SR criterion function

```
def SR_criterion(weight, data):
    """

    ---------------------------------------------------------------------

    | Output: Opposite Sharpe ratio to minimize it.                     |

    ---------------------------------------------------------------------

    | Inputs: -Weight (type ndarray numpy): Weight for portfolio        |
    |         -data (type dataframe pandas): Returns of stocks          |

    ---------------------------------------------------------------------

    """

    # Compute portfolio returns
    portfolio_return = np.multiply(data, np.transpose(weight))
    portfolio_return = portfolio_return.sum(axis=1)

    # Compute mean, volatility of the portfolio
    mean = np.mean(portfolio_return, axis=0)
    std = np.std(portfolio_return, axis=0)

    # Compute the opposite of the Sharpe ratio
    Sharpe = mean / std
    Sharpe = -Sharpe
    return Sharpe
```

Now, we can do the optimization problem as in the previous section. However, we will plot the results to compare the optimization methods in figure 3.8 and the portfolio weights in figure 3.7.

Figure 3.7: Weights allocation of the portfolio using SR criterion

Asset	Facebook	Netflix	Tesla
Weight	24.08%	48.01%	27.91%

As we can see, the optimization with the SR criterion takes Facebook stock for 24.08%, Netflix stock at 48.01%, and Tesla stock for 27.91%.

Figure 3.8: Cumulative returns of the portfolios on the test set

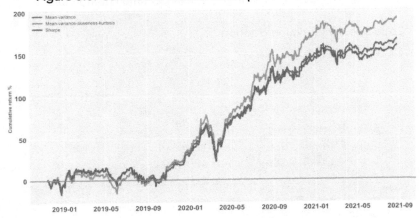

We can make the same interpretation as before. The portfolio follows the same trend but with a bit of variation.

3.3.2. Sortino criterion

In the last subsection, we have learned the maximum Sharpe ratio criterion. However, the Sharpe ratio has a big lousy point: it computes the volatility as the sum of the upward and downward volatility. Nevertheless, are we really against significant upward volatility when we are an investor? No, of course, because it is a synonym for a considerable profit. So, the enemy is just the downward volatility.

The Sortino ratio is an excellent metric because it derives from the Sharpe ratio, which only considers downward volatility. So, it allows us to understand the additional benefits for 1% more risk (only low risk). We can compute the Sortino ratio with the following formula:

$$Sortino = \frac{\mu - r_f}{\sigma_{downward}}$$

Where μ is the mean of the portfolio returns (annualized), $\sigma_{downward}$ is the downward volatility of the portfolio returns (annualized) and r_f is the risk-free asset (we set 0 for the risk-free assets because it is actually around this value).

So, as previously, we need to compute a function to minimize. In the following code part, we can find the SOR (Sortino) criterion function.

Code 3.9: SOR function criterion

```
def SOR_criterion(weight, data):
    """

    ----------------------------------------------------------------------
    | Output: Opposite Sortino ratio to do a minimization                 |
    ----------------------------------------------------------------------
    | Inputs: -Weight (type ndarray numpy): Wheight for portfolio         |
    |          -data (type dataframe pandas): Returns of stocks           |
    ----------------------------------------------------------------------
    """
    # Compute portfolio returns
    portfolio_return = np.multiply(data, np.transpose(weight))
    portfolio_return = portfolio_return.sum(axis=1)

    # Compute mean, volatility of the portfolio
    mean = np.mean(portfolio_return, axis=0)
    std = np.std(portfolio_return[portfolio_return < 0], axis=0) 1

    # Compute the opposite of the Sharpe ratio
    Sortino = mean / std
    Sortino = -Sortino

    return Sortino
```

1   To compute the downward volatility, we take all negative returns and calculate their standard deviation.

Now, we can do the optimization problem as in the previous section. However, we will plot the results to compare the optimization methods in figure 3.10 and the portfolio weights in figure 3.9.

Figure 3.9: Weights allocation of the portfolio using SOR criterion

Asset	Facebook	Netflix	Tesla
Weight	21.87%	49.85%	28.28%

As we can see, the optimization with the SOR criterion takes Facebook stock for 21.87%, Netflix stock at 49.85%, and Tesla stock for 28.28%.

The weight is also nearly the same. So, the portfolio will also be very similar to the others because the correlation between these three assets is high.

Figure 3.10: Cumulative returns of the portfolios on the test set

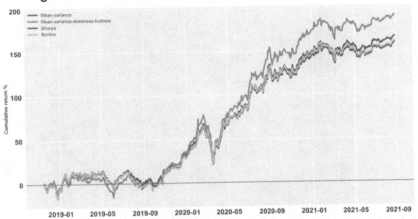

We can make the same interpretation as before. The portfolio follows the same trend but with a bit of variation.

Summary

- The specific risk is related to only one stock. In contrast, systemic risk is a macroeconomic risk that can affect all assets in the economy.

- Traditionally, we used approximation of the utility function to find criteria to maximize. For example, the mean-variance criterion and mean-variance skewness kurtosis criterion.

- Maximizing a function is equal to minimizing the opposite of the function.

- The Sharpe ratio quantifies the additional benefits for 1% more risk in the cost of total volatility.

- The Sortino ratio quantifies the additional benefits for 1% more risk in the low volatility cost.

- The key to a diversified portfolio is negatively correlated assets (we will discuss this in the next chapter about correlation).

Chapter 4: Tactical portfolio management

Static portfolio optimizations are an excellent way to optimize for a long-term investment. However, sometimes we need to deviate from our optimal static portfolio optimization using dynamic portfolio management. Moreover, dynamic portfolio methods can short some assets, and it can be advantageous to make benefits if the market goes up or down. To explain these methods, we will explain how a dynamic portfolio works, the moving average strategy, and the correlation strategy.

4.1. How dynamic methods works?

This section will explain how **tactical asset allocation (TAA)** works. To illustrate this notion, we will explain what short selling is, how to create a momentum factor and how to rebalance a dynamic portfolio.

4.1.1. Short a stock

Usually, in the **static portfolio strategies (SAA)**, we buy the stocks in suitable proportions. However, in the dynamic methods (TAA), we can also bet on the decrease of the stock, and it is called short selling. Short selling is usually used only with the TAA because the TAA has a tiny rebalancing interval: for example, one month, unlike SAA, which has a rebalancing interval very long, for example, three years. So, the TAA can capture the benefits when the price increase or decreases instead of the SAA, which allows us to bet only on the increase. Thus, when we buy a short-sell contract, we only bet on the decrease of the stock.

It is infrequent to short a stock directly. Usually, we will use a Contract for Difference (CFD) to bet to decrease the stock.
Reminder: We do not have access to the dividend with the CFD.

In figure 4.1, we can see the cash flows of a long contract (bet for the increase) and a short contract (bet for the decrease). P_1 is the cash flow at time 1, when purchasing the contract. For a long, we buy the stock in P_1. Thus, the cash flow is minus the stock price (with no transaction costs), and when we close the position, we have the actual price of the stock P_2. For the short contract, it is precisely the opposite. Indeed, when we buy the selling contract, we sell a lengthy contract that we do not already have but with the obligation to buy the stock later (in our example T_2). So, the benefits of an extended contract are P_2-P_1 and for the short contract P_1-P_2.

Figure 4.1: Cash flow for long and short contracts

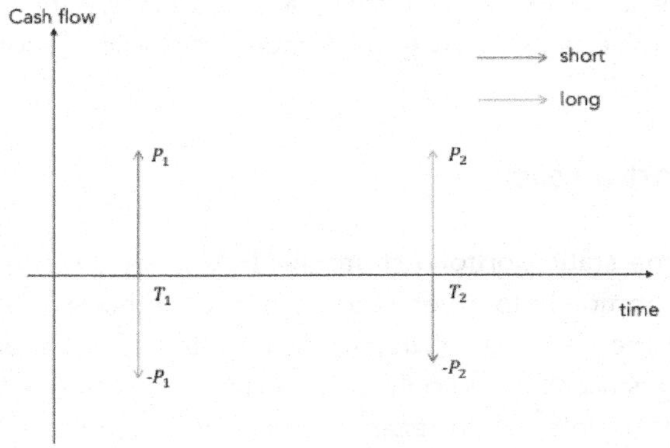

Cash flow

→ short

→ long

P_1 P_2

T_1 T_2 time

$-P_1$ $-P_2$

This figure shows the cash flow of a long and short contract from time T_2 to time T_2. In the figure, we can learn the following calculations, the benefits of an extended contract are P_2-P_1 and for the short contract P_1-P_2.

4.1.2. Momentum factor

At the beginning of a tactical asset allocation, we must choose a momentum factor. It is a value that we can build on the strategy. For example, in the next section, we will create a momentum factor with the autocorrelation of the asset. This factor is the strategy pillar. Indeed, if it is a good choice, we can do benefits, and if it is wrong, we will lose money.

We must understand that the momentum factor can be whatever we want. For example, we can create momentum using the interest rate growth, the country's inflation, the percentage of return over the last 12 months, etc.

We set a vector factor λ for this part to do all the necessary transformations. When we have this factor, we usually create a z-score, the normalization of the factor. We will put the formula of a z-score to highlight the process.

$$z_{\lambda i} = \frac{\lambda i - \mu_\lambda}{\sigma_\lambda}$$

Where λi is a value of the vector λ, μ_λ is the mean of the vector λ, and σ_λ is the standard deviation of the vector λ.

In this situation, the normalization of the data is not necessary. However, it is a good practice to keep in mind because it transforms our distribution into a mean 0 and standard deviation of 1.

When we have our z-score vector, we need to compute the median of the vector. Then, we will take a long position for all assets with a z-score superior to the median and a short position for all assets with a z-score inferior to the median. (This is our strategy, but we can take the threshold we want).

4.1.3. Rebalancing

The rebalancing of a TAA is an essential thing. Indeed, at this moment that the weights of each asset in the portfolio are determined. In the following examples, we will use allocation with the same weights for all assets to make things easier. The dynamic of the strategy will be only the sign (positive if we long and negative if we short).

Usually, we take the same weight to each asset and then combine the SAA and TAA portfolios following this equation[4].$porfolio = \alpha * SAA + (1 - \alpha) * TAA$ with $\alpha \in [0,1]$. Naturally, advanced technics changed each month's weight, but it will not be seen in the book.

Figure 4.2: Weights allocation of the TAA portfolio

Asset	Facebook	Netflix	Tesla
Weight	-33% / +33%	-33% / +33%	-33% / +33%

The weights of the assets as the same the only difference is that the contract can be long or short each month. So, the weight -33% or +33%.

4.2. Moving average strategy

This section will explain how to compute a tactical portfolio based on a moving average momentum. We will explain how moving averages work and how to make a dynamic portfolio using a moving average factor.

4.2.1. Moving average

This subsection will compute some moving averages to create the momentum factor in the second part. The moving average is the easiest to understand technical indicator. Indeed, it is a mean, but

---

[4] **Additional lecture** : Additional lecture :Tactical Asset Allocation (TAA), Adam BARONE

instead of doing the average on all the samples, we will create a vector of a mean of the n last day for each selected day..

It allows us to have a better comprehension of the stock behavior. We can build the moving average vector with the following formula.

$$mv_i = \frac{1}{n} \sum_{\Delta=i-n}^{i} x_\Delta$$

Where mv_i is the moving average at the index i, n is the window (the number of days you want to take to do the moving average), x is the asset's value.

Now, we will compute a moving average on the three previous assets for a window of 15 days with this code. Moreover, we will display the results in figure 4.3.

Code 4.1: Moving average computation

```
data["SMA15 FB"] = data["FB"].rolling(15).mean().shift(1)

data["SMA15 NFLX"] = data["NFLX"].rolling(15).mean().shift(1)

data["SMA15 TSLA"] = data["TSLA"].rolling(15).mean().shift(1)
```

In code 4.1, it is necessary to put a shift of 1. If one does not put it, we will forecast the value in t+15 in t+14 but using t+15 data. We will explain this later.

Figure 4.3: Assets with their simple moving average (SMA 15)

Date	FB	NFLX	TSLA	SMA 15 FB	SMA 15 NFLX	SMA 15 TSLA
06-11	27.01	9.00	5.82	29.84	9.63	5.89
06-12	27.40	9.00	5.93	29.01	9.56	5.91
06-13	27.27	8.97	5.95	28.65	9.48	5.93

The moving average is often used to understand the trend of the asset. Figure 4.4 shows the stock price with the SMA (simple moving average) of 15 and SMA of 60. So, it can be easy to understand the upward and downward trends.

Figure 4.4: Facebook stock price with SMA 15 and SMA 60

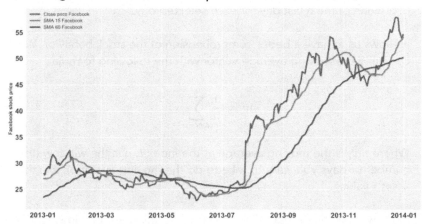

This figure shows the Facebook stock price with the SMA 15 and the SMA 60. When the trend is up, we see that the fast SMA is above the slow SMA and the opposite when the trend is down.

4.2.2. Moving average factor

In this subsection, we are going to build the moving average factor. Indeed, we will use the SMA for three months and SMA for 12 months of each stock (Facebook, Netflix, Tesla) to create a monthly signal to rebalance our portfolio.

We will use the same samples as in the previous chapter. We will use 70% of the data to create the strategy. Then, we will test it on the test set (the other 30%). The difference between the previous chapter and this one is that we keep the price in absolute value and not in variations. Then, we can compute the factor making the difference between the small and the long SMA. Moreover, we are computing the z-score in normalizing the factor. We can see how to do it in code 4.2 and the results in figure 4.5.

Code 4.2: Create the z-scores

```
list_tickers = ["FB", "NFLX", "TSLA"]

# We do a loop to create the SMAs for each asset

for col in list_tickers:

    data[f"pct {col}"] = data[col].pct_change(1)

    data[f"SMA3 {col}"] = data[col].rolling(3).mean().shift(1)
```

48

```
data[f"SMA12 {col}"] = data[col].rolling(12).mean().shift(1)
data[f"Momentum factor {col}"] = data[f"SMA3 {col}"] - \
data[f"SMA12 {col}"]


# Normalizing the zscore
split = int(0.7*len(data))
train_set = data.iloc[:split,:]
test_set = data.iloc[split:,:]


# Find the mean and std vectors
columns = [f"Momentum factor {col}" for col in list_tickers]
train_set_mean = train_set[columns].mean()
train_set_std = train_set[columns].std()


# Create the zscores
train_set[columns] = (train_set[columns]-train_set_mean)/
train_set_std
test_set[columns] = (test_set[columns]-train_set_mean)/
train_set_std1


# Find the medians
median = train_set[columns].median()
```

1   Computation of the test set z-scores using the train set's mean and std to avoid interference in the data. Usually, we cannot know the mean and std of this set because it is the future.

Figure 4.5: z-scores of the assets

Date	Momentum FB	Momentum NFLX	Momentum TSLA
06-01	-1.38	-0.36	0.16
07-01	-1.35	-0.39	0.68
08-01	-1.10	-0.42	1.23

In this figure, we can see the z-score momentum factor for each portfolio asset (Facebook, Netflix and Tesla).

4.2.3. Build the strategy

This subsection will show us how to build the tactical portfolio strategy using the moving average factor. We will do it using the z-scores calculated before.

First, we need to compute the signal of each asset if we take a long or short position in the coming month. Suppose the median of the z score is inferior to the z-score month. In that case, we take a short position the next month, and if the median of the z score is superior, we take a long position on the asset.

Code 4.3: Computation of signal and profit for SMA strategy

```
# Compute the signals and the profits
for i in range(len(columns)): 1

    # Initialize a new column for the signal
    test_set[f"signal {columns[i]}"] = 0 2

    # Signal is -1 if factor < median
    test_set.loc[test_set[f"{columns[i]}"]<median[i],
                 f"signal {columns[i]}"] = -1

    # Signal is 1 if factor > median
    test_set.loc[test_set[f"{columns[i]}"]>median[i],
                 f"signal {columns[i]}"] = 1

    # Compute the profit
    test_set[f"profit {columns[i]}"] = (test_set[f"signal
{columns[i]}"].shift(1)) * test_set[f"pct {list_tickers[i]}"] 3
```

1   Loop to compute the signal and profit for each asset.

2   Creation of a new column for the signal.

3   Add a shift to the signal because the signal tells us to enter in position. The profit signals today's and tomorrow's returns because we open the position at the close of the asset. If we take $signal_t$ * $return_t$ we will have excellent results but wrong.

We have also shifted to the signal because we see the next month if it is profitable when we have a signal. If we do not shift, we will make a massive profit because we will predict the past with the future, not the inverse. Now, let us see in figure 4.6 the results of this strategy.

Figure 4.6: Cumulative return of the tactical portfolio strategy

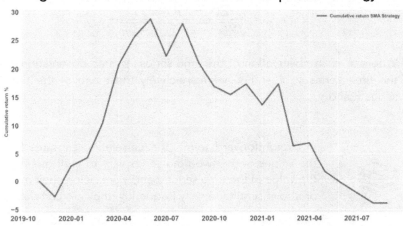

This figure shows that this strategy is not very profitable in the long term. Over the period, we have a drawdown of around 30% for a return of -3%.

4.3. Trend following strategy

This section will talk about the trend-following strategy. First, we need to explain the Pearson statistic correlation. Then, we will find the best asset for this strategy. Then, we will create a strategy with our trend following factor.

4.3.1. Correlation

This section will explain in detail how correlation works and why it is essential in this strategy. Indeed, the correlation will allow us to understand if there is some relation between the two-time series.

Correlation is an essential tool in finance. It allows us to understand the relationship between assets. However, many people use it in the wrong way. That is why we have a whole part dedicated to this notion. Many types of correlation exist, but the Pearson correlation is the most useful. It calculates the linear correlation between time series x and y with this formula:

$$\rho_{x,y} = \frac{\sum(x_i - \bar{x})(y_i - \bar{y})}{\sqrt{\sum(x_i - \bar{x})^2 \sum(y_i - \bar{y})^2}}$$

Where x_i is an observation of the time series , y_i is an observation of the time series y. $\bar{x}$ and $\bar{y}$ are respectively the mean of the time series x and y.

In straightforward terms, the correlation captures how the values of the two-time series vary to their means. If the value of the time series x and y are below their mean or above simultaneously frequently, they are correlated.

It is usually a good thing to take the time to analyze this equation a little bit. Indeed, as we can see, this formula computes the distance from the mean to the observation. So, as many assets have an upward trend, the correlation between the absolute price of the asset is positive. At the same time, the trend does represent the asset behavior. To solve this problem, we need to correlate the asset's variation percentage. Let us see some examples to be sure that the notion is understood.

In figure 4.7, we can see the value difference between the absolute value correlation and the variation percentage correlation.

Figure 4.7: Absolute value and return percentage correlation

Absolute value correlation

	Facebook	Netflix	Tesla
Facebook	1		
Netflix	0.94	1	
Tesla	0.76	0.74	1

Variation percentage correlation

	Facebook	Netflix	Tesla
Facebook	1		
Netflix	0.31	1	
Tesla	0.29	0.19	1

We can see that the difference between the absolute value and the variation percentage correlation is enormous. Some boxes are empty because the matrix is symmetric, which means the correlation between Facebook and Netflix is similar to the correlation between Netflix and Facebook.

Now, let us see how to interpret the Pearson correlation:

- **-1 < corr < 0**: There is a negative correlation between the two assets. That means if the first increase, the second has more chance to decrease. More Pearson correlation is close to -1 more the chance of decreasing is high.

- **Corr = 0**: There is no correlation. That means if one increases or decreases, we can say nothing about the behavior of the other asset.

- **0 < corr < 1**: There is a positive correlation between the two assets. That means if the first increase the second has more chance to increase. More Pearson correlation is close to 1 more, the probability of increasing is high.

If the assets have a robust correlation, they will often dry up in the same direction but **not necessarily with the same intensity.**

4.3.2. Trend following factor

In this subsection, we have to change the assets a little. We probably ask why, for this last strategy, we must change the asset instead. We said that we take only the same to compare the strategy in the next chapter. True, but this strategy has a different process from the others.

This strategy uses the 12 of last month's returns to create a factor investment. Moreover, the position is rebalancing each month. However, to find the best asset, we need to use the correlation on many assets to find the bests. So, naturally, the best assets are not the same as the previous ones.

To find the best assets, we will take ten assets, but we can take more to have a better choice. Furthermore, we compute the autocorrelation between the 12 last month and the one next month to find the best asset for the strategy on the train set. That means we search for the assets with the best correlation between the lookback period and the hold period (you can also find the best lookback and hold period with this technique).

Code 4.4: Best asset selection

```
# Compute the lookback and hold period
for col in list_:
    data[f"pct+1 {col}"] = data[f"{col}"].pct_change(-1) 1
    data[f"pct-12 {col}"] = data[f"{col}"].pct_change(12) 2


# Normalizing the zscore
split = int(0.7*len(data))
train_set = data.iloc[:split,:]
test_set = data.iloc[split:,:]



# Compute the correlation
corr = []
for col in list_:
    cor = train_set[[f"pct-12 {col}", f"pct+1
{col}"]].corr().values[0][1]


    corr.append(cor)
correlation = pd.DataFrame(corr, index=list_, columns=["Corr"])3
correlation.sort_values(by="Corr", ascending=False)
```

1   Computation of the hold period return (1 month).

2   Computation of the lookback period return (12 months).

3   List_ is a list containing all the assets that we want to test for the strategy.

Figure 4.8: Best assets with the previous asset correlation

Asset	INTC	GOOG	PYPL	TSLA	FB	NFLX
Corr	0.29	0.24	0.19	0.17	0.09	0.07

This figure shows the correlation between the lookback and holds period for the three best and previous assets.

Now, we have three assets (Intel, Google, and PayPal) to compute a strategy. First, we need to compute the z-score to find the signal investment. Now, we have three assets to compute a strategy. First, we must compute the z score to find the signal investment. Then as previously, we will take a short position if the z score is below the median and take a long position if the z score is above the median.

Code 4.5: Create the z-scores

```python
best = ["PYPL", "INTC", "GOOG"]


# Find the mean and std vectors
columns = [f"pct-12 {col}" for col in best]
train_set_mean = train_set[columns].mean()
train_set_std = train_set[columns].std()


# Create the zscores
train_set[columns] = (train_set[columns] - train_set_mean) /
train_set_std
test_set[columns] = (test_set[columns] - train_set_mean) /
train_set_std


# Find the medians
median = train_set[columns].median()
```

4.3.3. Compute the strategy

In this part, we will compute the strategy. To do it, it is precisely the same code as for the moving average strategy. Now, let us see in figure 4.9 the results of this strategy.

Unlike the SMA strategy after the corona crisis, we can see a decrease in the cumulative return. It can be explained by the fact that the crisis misleads the 12 last month's returns.

Figure 4.9: Performance of the trend returns strategy

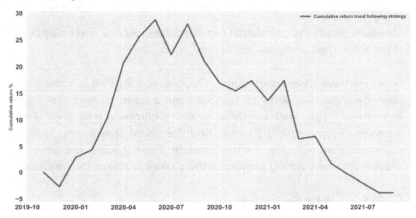

In this figure, we can see the profit of the trend return strategy.

Summary

- A short position allows us to bet on the decrease of a stock.

- Tactical portfolio strategies are an excellent way to capture benefits when the market increases or decreases.

- TAA portfolio is helpful to correct the imperfection of the SAA. So, we need to combine both to have a good portfolio.

- Moving average is an excellent way to have a more significant average.

- Correlation is an excellent way to understand the relation between two behavior stocks.

Chapter 5: Risk management and backtesting

This chapter will backtest some previous investment strategies using risk management metrics and other indicators. We will begin with the best-known backtest metrics like beta, alpha, Sharpe ratio, Sortino ratio, and drawdown. Then, we will explain how to perform risk analysis using VaR, cVaR, and Risk contributions. Moreover, we will automatize this analysis to apply it to later strategies.

5.1. The backtesting metrics

This section will discuss CPAM metrics to understand the relationship between our strategy and the market. Then, we will compute the drawdown of our strategies to understand how much time we lose money over the period when we follow a strategy.

5.1.1. The CAPM metrics

First, we will talk about the CAPM[5] metrics. Indeed, CAPM is the most famous model for portfolio management and gives us some exciting metrics: the beta and the alpha.

The beta metric of a stock highlights the relation between the market represented by a market stock index like S&P 500 and the portfolio. For example, a beta of 1.15 implies that if the market has a variation of 1%, the portfolio varies to 1.15%. It can be considered a metric of systemic portfolio risk. It is computed using the following formula:

$$\beta_s = \frac{Cov(r_s, r_m)}{Var(r_m)}$$

r_s is the asset's return and r_m is the market index's return.
When we compute the beta, you will be in one of these situations:

---

[5] **Additional lecture:** https://en.wikipedia.org/wiki/Capital_asset_pricing_model

- β_s < 1: It means that the portfolio is less volatile than the market, which is good because it does not have a significant systemic risk.
- β_s = 1: The portfolio moves in the same market proportion. Suppose the market moves to 1%, and the portfolio moves to 1%.

- β_s > 1: The portfolio is more volatile than the market and has a significant systemic risk.

Now, let us create a function to compute the beta of a portfolio. (In this example, the benchmark will be the S&P 500 and his Yahoo symbol is "^GSPC").

Code 5.1: beta ratio function

```
def beta_function(portfolio, ben = "^GSPC"):1

    """

    ----------------------------------------------------------------
    | Output: Beta CAPM metric                                     |
    ----------------------------------------------------------------
    | Inputs: - portfolio (type dataframe pandas): Returns of the portfolio |
    |         - ben (type string): Name of the benchmark           |
    ----------------------------------------------------------------

    """


    # Import the benchmark
    benchmark = yf.download(ben)["Adj Close"].pct_change(1).dropna()


    # Concat the asset and the benchmark
    join = pd.concat((portfolio, benchmark), axis=1).dropna()2


    # Covariance between the asset and the benchmark
    cov = np.cov(join, rowvar=False)[0][1] 3


    # Compute the variance of the benchmark
    var = np.cov(join, rowvar=False)[1][1]


    return cov/var
```

1   The default setting for the benchmark is S&P 500 (^GSPC), but we can put all indices that we want depending on the market we want to take.

2   Creation of a data frame with the strategy and benchmark returns to delete the days that are not in the two-time series.

3   It is essential to specify *rowvar=False* because, without that, python will consider that each row represents a time series instead of each column. Thus, if we do not set this parameter, we will have a bad result.

 We have computed the benchmark variance using the covariance matrix because the diagonal values are the variance of the assets.

With this function, we have obtained a beta at 1.08 for the portfolio using the mean-variance criterion. It means that when the market (S&P 500) varies by 1%, the portfolio varies by 1.08%.
Now let us talk about the alpha metric. It allows us to understand if a portfolio outperforms or underperforms the benchmark. For example, suppose we have a portfolio with an alpha of 0.0115. In that case, the portfolio outperforms the benchmark by 1.15%, considering the portfolio's returns and risk. It can be computed using the following formula:

$$\alpha_s = E[r_s] - r_f - \beta_s(E[r_m] - r_f)$$

Where $E[r_s]$ is the mean of the asset's return and $E[r_m]$ is the of the market index returns, r_f the return of the risk-free asset and β_s the asset's beta.

 When we compute a mean of return, volatility, Sharpe ratio, etc. We need to annualize the values (always). Because if we want to compare some strategies with different time frames, it can be very hard.

The risk-free asset is very close to 0%, even negative in some situations. So, it is preferred to set it at 0% to facilitate computation and comprehension.

When we compute the alpha, we will be in one of these situations:

- $\alpha_s < 0$: That means that the portfolio underperforms the benchmark. This is not a good thing because it would have been a better investment if we had just bought the benchmark.

- $\alpha_s = 0$: That means that the portfolio neither underperforms nor outperforms the benchmark, this is not good because it means that if we had just bought the benchmark, it is the same couple risk-return.

- $\alpha_s > 0$: That means that the portfolio outperforms the benchmark, and this is a good thing. It means that we had a better investment than the benchmark.

Code 5.2: alpha ratio function

```
def alpha_function(portfolio, ben = "^GSPC", timeframe= 252):
    """

    ---------------------------------------------------------------------

    | Output: Alpha CAPM metric                                         |

    ---------------------------------------------------------------------

    | Inputs: - portfolio (type dataframe pandas): Returns of the portfolio  |

    |         - ben (type string): Name of the benchmark                |

    |         - timeframe (type int): annualization factor             |

    ---------------------------------------------------------------------

    """


    # Import the benchmark
    benchmark = yf.download(ben)["Adj Close"].pct_change(1).dropna()


    # Concat the asset and the benchmark
    join = pd.concat((portfolio, benchmark), axis=1).dropna()
```

```
# Compute the beta
beta = beta_function(portfolio_return_MV, ben=ben) 1


mean_stock_return = join.iloc[:,0].mean()*timeframe
mean_market_return = join.iloc[:,1].mean()*timeframe
return mean_stock_return - beta*mean_market_return
```

1   Utilization of beta_function created before to compute the beta.

 We have set a new parameter named timeframe to allow us to manage the annualization of the data. Indeed, we cannot multiply by the same factor if we have monthly and daily returns. Here, the timeframe is 252 because there are daily returns.

We obtained an alpha of 35% for the portfolio using the mean-variance criterion with this function. It means that when the portfolio outperforms by 35%, the benchmark.

5.1.2. Sharpe and Sortino

In this part, we will discuss some metrics we have already seen. Indeed, these metrics are used in chapter 3: Sharpe and Sortino ratios. However, we will go deeper into the subject to understand these metrics.

Let us talk about the Sharpe ratio. This metric is very used in finance; as we said before, it allows us to understand the additional benefits of 1% more risk.

$$Sharpe = \frac{\mu - r_f}{\sigma}$$

Where μ is the mean of the portfolio returns (annualized), σ is the volatility of the portfolio returns (annualized) and r_f is the risk-free asset (we set 0 for the risk-free assets because it is actually around this value).

 To annualize the volatility, we need to multiply the volatility by the square root of the annualization factor. For example, if we want to annualize daily volatility, we do $\sigma_{daily} * \sqrt{252}$.

When we compute the Sharpe ratio, we will be in one of these situations:

- **sharpe < 0**: This is not a good investment. We took some risks, but we have a negative expected return on our portfolio.

- **0 < sharpe < 1**: This is a good investment. We have a positive expected return, but the risk we take is higher than the return.
- **sharpe > 1**: This is an excellent investment. We have a positive expected return but with riskless importance than the returns.

Code 5.3: Sharpe ratio function

```
def sharpe_function(portfolio, timeframe= 252):
    """

    -----------------------------------------------------------------

    | Output: Sharpe ratio metric                                    |

    -----------------------------------------------------------------

    | Inputs: - portfolio (type dataframe pandas): Returns of the portfolio   |
    |         - timeframe (type int): annualization factor           |

    -----------------------------------------------------------------

    """

    mean = portfolio.mean() * timeframe

    std = portfolio.std() * np.sqrt(timeframe)


    return mean/std
```

Using the mean-variance criterion with this function, we obtained a Sharpe ratio of 1.37 for the portfolio. This is an outstanding portfolio because 1% of additional risk gives 1.37% of return.

Now, let us talk about the Sortino ratio. The Sortino ratio is an excellent metric because it derives from the Sharpe ratio, which only considers downward volatility. So, it allows us to understand the additional benefits for 1% more of low risk. We can compute the Sortino ratio with the following formula:

$$Sortino = \frac{\mu - r_f}{\sigma_{downward}}$$

Where μ is the mean of the portfolio returns (annualized), $\sigma_{downward}$ is the downward volatility of the portfolio returns (annualized), and r_f is the risk-free asset (we set 0 for the risk-free assets because it is actually around this value).

The Sortino ratio can be better than the Sharpe ratio because it is only sensible to downward volatility. Thus, it is more representative of what the investor wants.

When we compute the Sortino ratio, we will be in one of these situations:

- **sortino < 0**: This is not a good investment. We took some low risk, but we have a negative expected return on our portfolio.
- **0 < sortino < 1**: This is a good investment. we have a positive expected return, but the low risk we take is higher than the return.
- **sortino > 1**: This is an excellent investment. We have a positive expected return but a less crucial downward risk than the returns.

The only difference between Sharpe and Sortino ratios is how to compute the risk. One chooses the volatility and another the downward volatility.

Code 5.4: Sortino ratio function

```
def sortino_function(portfolio, timeframe= 252):
    """

    ----------------------------------------------------------------------
    | Output: Sortino ratio metric                                       |
    ----------------------------------------------------------------------

    | Inputs: - portfolio (type dataframe pandas): Returns of the portfolio  |
    |          - timeframe (type int): annualization factor              |
    ----------------------------------------------------------------------

    """


    # Take downward values
    portfolio = portfolio.values
    downward = portfolio[portfolio<0]


    mean = portfolio.mean() * timeframe
    std = downward.std() * np.sqrt(timeframe)


    return mean/std
```

With this function, we have obtained a Sortino ratio of 1.87 for the portfolio using the mean-variance criterion. This is an excellent portfolio, and 1% of additional downward risk gives 1.87% of return.

5.1.3. Drawdown

In this part, we will talk about drawdown. It is one of the best metrics for a backtest. Indeed, it allows us to understand the significant loss we suffer. It gives us the most prominent loss if we enter a position at the worst time of this period. Now, it can be complicated to understand, but it is a straightforward thing. Let us see. First, we need to explain the formula to compute the drawdown:

$$\delta_i = \frac{\varphi_i}{\phi_i} - 1$$

Where δ_i is the drawdown at the time i, φ_i the cumulative product return at the time i and ϕ_i is the running max at the time i for i in *[portfolio start date: portfolio end date]*.

Code 5.5: drawdown vector function

```
def drawdown_function(portfolio):

    """

    -----------------------------------------------------------------
    | Output: Drawdown                                              |
    -----------------------------------------------------------------

    | Inputs: - portfolio (type dataframe pandas): Returns of the portfolio  |
    -----------------------------------------------------------------

    """

    # Compute the cumulative product returns
    cum_rets = (portfolio+1).cumprod()1


    # Compute the running max
    running_max = np.maximum.accumulate(cum_rets.dropna())2
    running_max[running_max < 1] = 1


    # Compute the drawdown
    drawdown = ((cum_rets)/running_max - 1)3


    return drawdown
```

1   Computation of the cumulative return using the compounding interest (you can read the annex about this subject) because it is more sensible to the losses.

2   Computation of the cumulative max value.

3   Compute the drawdown which is the ratio between the cumulative return and the cumulative max.

Then, we can compute the drawdown of the mean-variance portfolio. We can display the drawdown of the portfolio in figure 5.1.

Figure 5.1: Drawdown of the mean-variance portfolio

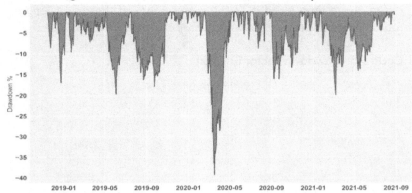

This figure shows the drawdown of the mean-variance portfolio computes in chapter 3 of this book.

As we can see, the max drawdown is around 40% during the corona crisis. It is because it is a long-only strategy. Except for this period, the drawdown is around 15%. It means that if we enter in position with this portfolio just before the crisis, we have lost 40% of our capital in 1 month. However, after May, we have found our capital at 100%.

We can compute the cumulative return of the portfolio using the cumulative sum or the product sum. The cumulative sum is used for the fixed lot strategy and the cumulative product for the auto lot strategy.

5.2. Risk management metrics

In this section, we will talk about the risk management metrics. We will see the best-known risk management metric, the Value at Risk (VaR). Then we will see a derivative of this metric: the conditional value at risk (cVaR). Moreover, we will learn how to compute the risk contribution of each asset in the portfolio.

5.2.1. Value at risk (VaR)

In this subsection, we discuss Value at Risk (VaR). It is an excellent risk metric. Indeed, it allows us to understand how much we lose in the worst case, considering an error threshold. First, let us see one formula to compute the VaR (there are many, and we will see only one).

$$VaR_\theta = \mu + \sigma \, \phi^{-1}(\theta)$$

Where μ is the returns of the portfolio, σ the volatility of the portfolio, θ the error threshold and ϕ the CDF of N(0,1).

The VaR depends on the timeframe we use. We will have a worse daily loss if we use daily return distribution. So, if we want the yearly worse loss, we need to annualize the returns and the volatility before.

The reflection with the inverse of the CDF function is a little bit complicated. We can explain the concept easier in figure 5.2.

Figure 5.2: VaR explanation

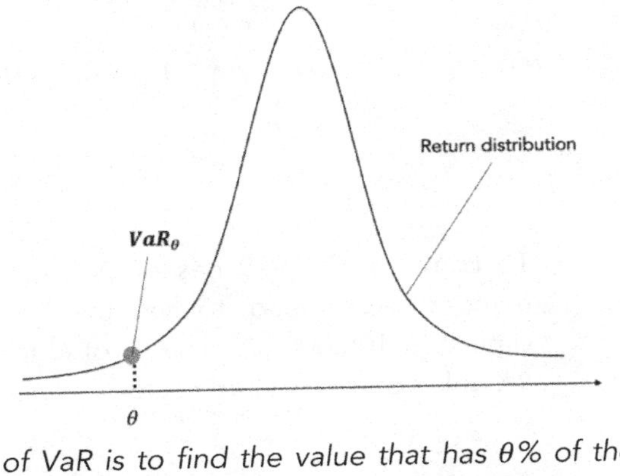

Return distribution

VaR_θ

θ

The objective of VaR is to find the value that has $\theta\%$ of the values above it. For example, if theta is equal to 5%, the VaR is the value with 5% of the returns ordered above it.

Code 5.6: VaR function

```
def VaR_function(theta, mu, sigma):
    """

    ---------------------------------------------------------------
    | Output: VaR                                                 |
    ---------------------------------------------------------------
    | Inputs: - theta (type float): % error threshold            |
    |         - mu (type float): portfolio expected return        |
    |         - sigma (type float): portfolio volatility          |
    ---------------------------------------------------------------

    """
    # Number of simulations
    n = 100000

    # Find the values for theta% error threshold
    t = int(n*theta)

    # Create a vector with n simulations of the normal law
    vec = pd.DataFrame(np.random.normal(mu, sigma, size=(n,)),
                       columns = ["Simulations"])

    # Orderer the values and find the theta% value
    var = vec.sort_values(by="Simulations").iloc[t].values[0]

    return var
```

To compute the VaR easier, we have used the large number law. Indeed, to find the θ% value, we have simulated 100,000 simulations of N (μ, σ) and take the θ% value of the ordered vector.

Using this function, we can find the VaR for the mean-variance portfolio. Indeed, for this portfolio, we found a VaR of 3.87% for a day, 13.61% for a month, and 7.02% for a year. It means that in the 5% of the worst-case, we can lose more than 3.87% by day, 13.61% by month, and 7.02% by year with this strategy.

The Var is an exciting metric. However, it does not consider the extremity (whether they are much or not) of the values below the VaR. To do it, we need to compute the cVaR.

5.2.2. Conditional Value at risk (cVaR)

This subsection will discuss the conditional Value at risk (cVaR[6]). It is a derivative of the VaR. Indeed, this metric is in the same mind as the VaR but takes extreme values into account, unlike the ordinary VaR.

Indeed, the cVaR does a mean of each value below the VaR. So, if there are extreme values, they will consider them. Let us put the formula of the cVaR before a schema in figure 5.3 to understand easier:

$$cVaR_\theta = \mu + \sigma \; \frac{\varphi(\phi^{-1}(\theta))}{1 - \theta}$$

Where μ is the returns of the portfolio, σ the volatility of the portfolio, θ the error threshold, φ the PDF (Partial Distribution Function) of N(0,1) and ϕ the CDF (Cumulative Distribution Function) of N(0,1).

Figure 5.3: cVaR explanation

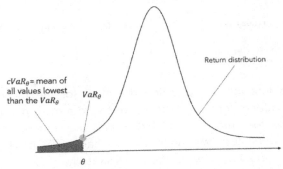

In this figure, we can see how to compute the cVaR. Indeed, it is the mean of the values below the VaR.

---

[6] **Additional lecture:** Optimization of conditional value-at-risk, R. Tyrrell Rockafellar

Code 5.7: Function for cVaR

```
def cVaR_function(theta, mu, sigma):
    """

    ------------------------------------------------------------------
    | Output: cVaR                                                    |
    ------------------------------------------------------------------
    | Inputs: - theta (type float): % error threshold                |
    |           - mu (type float): portfolio expected return          |
    |           - sigma (type float): portfolio volatility            |
    ------------------------------------------------------------------

    """

    # Number of simulations
    n = 100000

    # Find the values for theta% error threshold
    t = int(n*theta)

    # Create a vector with n simulations of the normal law
    vec = pd.DataFrame(np.random.normal(mu, sigma, size=(n,)),
                       columns = ["Simulations"])

    # Orderer the values and find the theta% value
    cvar
=vec.sort_values(by="Simulations").iloc[0:t,:].mean().values[0]

    return cvar
```

Using this function, we can find the cVaR for the mean-variance portfolio. Indeed, for this portfolio, we found a cVaR of 4.87% for a day, 18.28% for a month, and 24.20% for a year. It means that in the 5% of the worst-case, we can lose more than 4.87% by day, 18.28% by month, and 24.20% by year with this strategy.

 I am using the cVaR. It is most interesting because it considers significant money losses below the VaR.

5.2.3. Contribution risk

Risk contribution is an interesting metric because it allows us to understand the percentage of risk for each asset. Indeed, this metric lets us know which asset adds the most risk to the portfolio.

To compute the risk contribution, we need to have the beta of the assets and the weight of each asset in the portfolio. Let us see how to compute with the formula:

$$\lambda_i = \beta_i * \omega_i$$

Where λ_i is the contribution to the risk of each asset, β_i is the beta of the assets and ω_i is the weight of the asset i in the portfolio.

To computes the percentage of each risk asset in the portfolio we need to divide the λ_i by the sum $(\sum \lambda_i)$ to have a base of 100%.

Code 5.8: Risk contribution function

```
def CR_function(weights,database, ben="^GSPC"):

    """ -----------------------------------------------------------------

    | Output: Contribution risk metric                                  |

    -----------------------------------------------------------------

    | Inputs: - weights (type 1d array numpy): weights of the portfolio  |

    |         - database (type dataframe pandas): Returns of the asset   |

    |         - ben (type string): Name of the benchmark                 |

    -----------------------------------------------------------------

    """

    # Find the number of the asset in the portfolio

    l = len(weights)


    # Compute the risk contribution of each asset

    crs = []

    for i in range(l):

        cr = beta_function(data.iloc[:,i]) * weights[i]

        crs.append(cr)
```

71

```
return crs/np.sum(crs)  # Normalizing by the sum of the risk
contribution
```

Using this function, we can find the risk contribution of each asset. Indeed, Facebook represents 31.04% of the portfolio's risk, Netflix 30.61%, and Tesla 38.34%. We can also represent these values in a graphic like in figure 5.4.

Figure 5.4: Risk contribution graphic

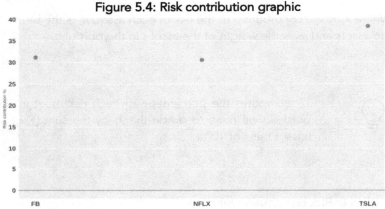

In this figure, we can see each asset's risk contribution to the portfolio's risk.

Now, we have the necessary metrics to backtest a strategy. In the next section, we will create a function to apply easily to each strategy.

5.3. Automate the analysis

This section will create a backtesting function, and we will backtest all the previous strategies.

5.3.1. Create a function

In this subsection, we will retake sections 5.1 and 5.2 to create a function, which will be used in the next chapter. Let us see the code and explain some details.

Code 5.9: Function for backtesting

```python
def    backtest(weights,    database,    ben="^GSPC",    timeframe=252,
CR=False):
    """

    ---------------------------------------------------------------------

    | Output: Beta CAPM metric                                          |

    ---------------------------------------------------------------------

    | Inputs: - weights (type 1d array numpy): weights of the portfolio |
    |         - database (type dataframe pandas): Returns of the asset  |
    |         - ben (type string): Name of the benchmark               |
    |         - timeframe (type int): annualization factor             |

    ---------------------------------------------------------------------

    """

    # Compute the portfolio
    portfolio = np.multiply(database,np.transpose(weights))
    portfolio = portfolio.sum(axis=1)
    columns = database.columns
    columns = [col for col in columns]


    #################### COMPUTE THE BETA ######################
    # Import the benchmark
    benchmark = yf.download(ben)["Adj Close"].pct_change(1).dropna()


    # Concat the asset and the benchmark
    join = pd.concat((portfolio, benchmark), axis=1).dropna()


    # Covariance between the asset and the benchmark
    cov = np.cov(join, rowvar=False)[0][1]


    # Compute the variance of the benchmark
    var = np.cov(join, rowvar=False)[1][1]
```

```
beta = cov/var


###################### COMPUTE THE ALPHA ######################
# Mean of returns for the asset
mean_stock_return = join.iloc[:,0].mean()*timeframe

# Mean of returns for the market
mean_market_return = join.iloc[:,1].mean()*timeframe

# Alpha
alpha = mean_stock_return - beta*mean_market_return


###################### COMPUTE THE SHARPE ######################
mean = portfolio.mean() * timeframe
std = portfolio.std() * np.sqrt(timeframe)
Sharpe = mean/std


###################### COMPUTE THE SORTINO ######################
downward = portfolio[portfolio<0]
std_downward = downward.std() * np.sqrt(timeframe)
Sortino = mean/std_downward


###################### COMPUTE THE DRAWDOWN ######################
# Compute the cumulative product returns
cum_rets = (portfolio+1).cumprod()

# Compute the running max
running_max = np.maximum.accumulate(cum_rets.dropna())
running_max[running_max < 1] = 1

# Compute the drawdown
drawdown = ((cum_rets)/running_max - 1)
min_drawdon = -drawdown.min()
```

```python
##################### COMPUTE THE VaR ##########################
theta = 0.01
# Number of simulations
n = 100000

# Find the values for theta% error threshold
t = int(n*theta)

# Create a vector with n simulations of the normal law
vec = pd.DataFrame(np.random.normal(mean, std, size=(n,)),
                   columns = ["Simulations"])

# Orderer the values and find the theta% value
VaR = -vec.sort_values(by="Simulations").iloc[t].values[0]

##################### COMPUTE THE cVaR #########################
cVaR = -vec.sort_values(by="Simulations").iloc[0:t,:].mean()\
.values[0]

##################### COMPUTE THE RC ##########################
if CR:
    # Find the number of the asset in the portfolio
    l = len(weights)

    # Compute the risk contribution of each asset
    crs = []
    for i in range(l):
        cr = beta_function(data.iloc[:,i]) * weights[i]
        crs.append(cr)

    crs = crs/np.sum(crs)  # Normalizing by the sum of the risk
contribution

##################### PLOT THE RESULTS #########################
print(f""" ------------------------------------------------------
 Portfolio: {columns}
 ------------------------------------------------------

 Beta : {np.round(beta, 3)} \t Alpha: {np.round(alpha, 3)} \t \
```

75

```
Sharpe: {np.round(Sharpe, 3)} \t Sortino: {np.round(Sortino, 3)}

------------------------------------------------------------------

VaR : {np.round(VaR, 3)} \t cVaR: {np.round(cVaR, 3)} \t \
VaR/cVaR: {np.round(cVaR/VaR, 3)}

------------------------------------------------------------------
""")
plt.figure(figsize=(10,6))
plt.plot(portfolio.cumsum())
plt.title("CUMULTATIVE RETURN", size=15)
plt.show()


plt.figure(figsize=(10,6))
plt.fill_between(drawdown.index, drawdown*100, 0, color="#E95751")
plt.title("DRAWDOWN", size=15)
plt.show()


if CR:
  plt.figure(figsize=(10,6))
  plt.scatter(columns, crs, linewidth=3, color = "#B96553")
  plt.axhline(0, color="#53A7B9")
  plt.grid(axis="x")
  plt.title("RISK CONTRIBUTION PORTFOLIO", size=15)
  plt.xlabel("Assets")
  plt.ylabel("Risk contribution")
  plt.show()
```

 Incorporating a parameter that displays or does not display specific metrics avoids needing to create many functions.

Figure 5.5: Backtest for the mean-variance portfolio

```
Portfolio: ['FB', 'NFLX', 'TSLA']

Beta: 1.066    Alpha: 35.45 %    Sharpe: 1.51    Sortino: 2.034

VaR: 30.74 %    cVaR: 42.98 %    VaR/cVaR: 1.398    drawdown: 39.27 %
```

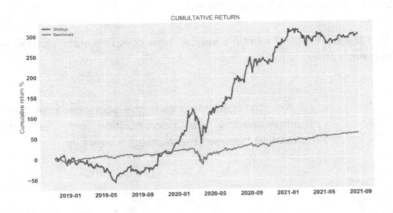

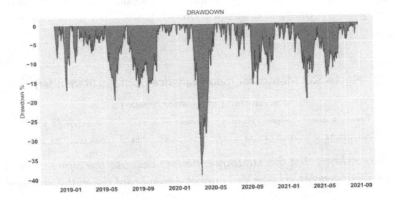

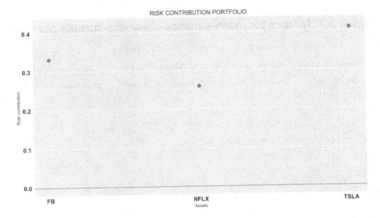

This figure shows the backtest of the mean-variance strategy with metrics and some plots to better understand the portfolio behavior.

5.3.2. Analyze static portfolio

With the backtesting function, we can now compare static portfolios with each other.

All the strategies are nearly the same because these strategies allow the long position only, and the correlation between these assets is very high.

It would be helpful to find assets with a negative correlation of returns. It would provide excellent portfolio diversification.

Figure 5.6: Metrics for mean-variance portfolio (Reminder)

```
          Portfolio: ['FB', 'NFLX', 'TSLA']

  Beta: 1.066    Alpha: 35.45 %    Sharpe: 1.51    Sortino: 2.034

  VaR: 30.74 %   cVaR: 42.98 %     VaR/cVaR: 1.398  drawdown: 39.27 %
```

This figure shows that this strategy is perfect because the alpha is equal to 35.45%. However, a huge VaR implies a significant risk in this strategy.

Figure 5.7: Metrics for mean-variance-skewness-kurtosis portfolio

```
          Portfolio: ['FB', 'NFLX', 'TSLA']

  Beta: 1.136    Alpha: 47.35 %    Sharpe: 1.547   Sortino: 2.105

  VaR: 33.36 %   cVaR: 47.59 %     VaR/cVaR: 1.427  drawdown: 44.24 %
```

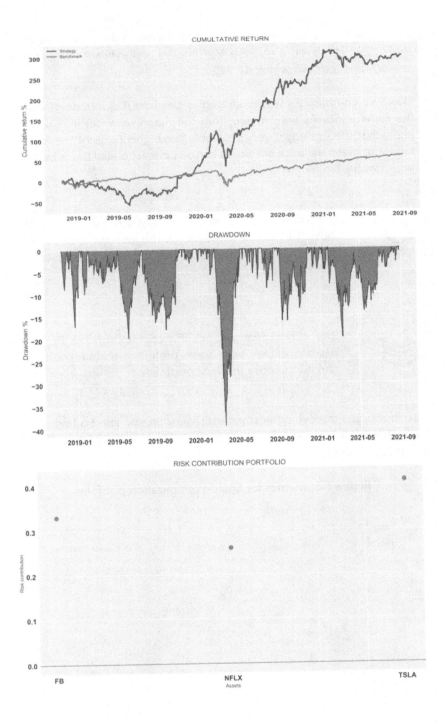

This figure shows that this strategy is good because the alpha is equal to 47.35%. However, a massive VaR implies a significant risk in this strategy and a drawdown at 44.24%.

Now, we compare these two strategies because it is strategies with the same mind. As we can see from the mean-variance, all metrics imply that the strategy is very profitable but highly risky. At the same time, the mean-variance skewness kurtosis portfolio also has a better return with a higher risk.

With these metrics, we cannot say which strategy is the best. This choice depends on the investor. Indeed, if it likes risky investment, it will choose the second, otherwise the first.

The only differences are the contribution risk of each asset. So, if we have some preferences in an asset, we can also choose the best portfolio.

Let us discuss the two other static strategies, Sharpe and Sortino portfolios. We can see in figures 5.8 and 5.9 the metrics of the respective strategy.

Figure 5.8: Metrics for Sharpe optimization portfolio

Portfolio: ['FB', 'NFLX', 'TSLA']

Beta: 1.048	Alpha: 31.28 %	Sharpe: 1.266	Sortino: 1.772
VaR: 40.37 %	cVaR: 53.62 %	VaR/cVaR: 1.328	drawdown: 35.52%

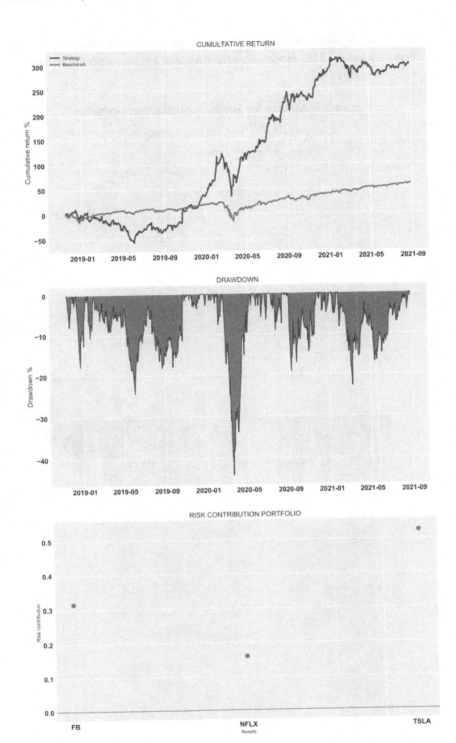

In this figure, we can say that this strategy is excellent because the alpha equals 40.37%. However, a massive VaR implies a significant risk in this strategy.

Figure 5.9: Metrics for Sortino optimization portfolio

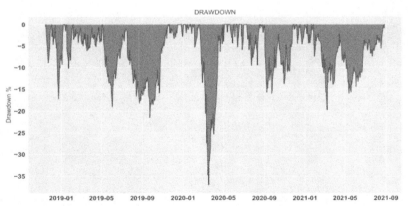

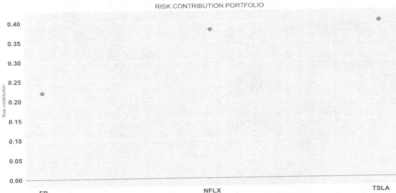

This figure shows that this strategy is excellent because the alpha is equal to 41.13%. However, a massive VaR implies a significant risk in this strategy.

As we can see, the two strategies have nearly the same metrics. We cannot say if one or the other is better. The only difference is the risk in each asset. If we prefer investing in Netflix stock and believe in this stock, we take the Sortino portfolio. However, if we prefer Tesla, we choose the Sharpe portfolio, for example.

5.3.3. Analyze dynamic portfolio

In this part, we talk about the analysis of dynamic portfolios. Indeed, they were awful compared to the static portfolio.

But why? There are several answers to this question. First, it was critical to understand that our dynamic portfolio is a fundamental strategy.

Also, we did not make asset selection for the first strategy with the SMA. The strategies are also straightforward, but the objective was to enter smoothly into the field of long-short strategies. So, we will see in the following chapters how to create short-term algorithmic trading strategies that work much better than these. Let us see the results of these strategies in figure 5.10 and figure 5.11.

Figure 5.10: Metrics for SMA optimization portfolio

Beta: -0.917   Alpha: 13.58 %   Sharpe: 0.4   Sortino: 0.929

83

VaR: 64.9 %   cVaR: 76.31 %   VaR/cVaR: 1.176   drawdown: 44.05 %

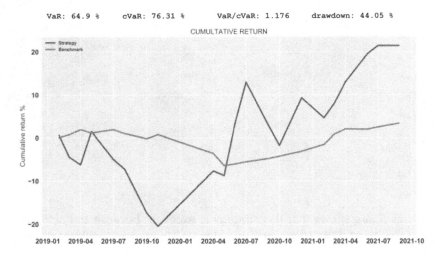

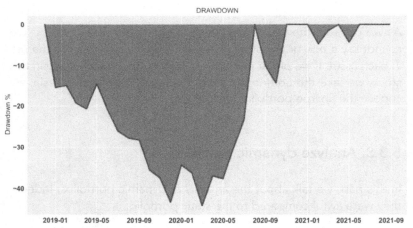

*This figure shows that this strategy is not good because the alpha
equals 13.58%, and the VaR is at 64% annually. The Sharpe ratio is
meager (0.40).*

Figure 5.11: Metrics for Trend returns optimization portfolio

Beta: -2.118   Alpha: -1.31 %   Sharpe: -0.058   Sortino: -0.092

VaR: 40.74 %   cVaR: 46.4 %   VaR/cVaR: 1.134   drawdown: 27.7%

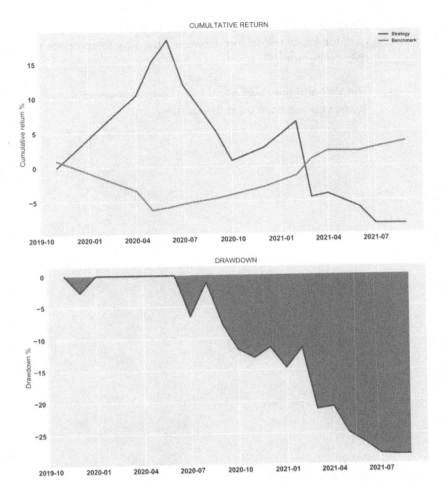

This figure shows that this strategy is not good because the alpha equals -1.53%, but the VaR is at 40%, and the Sharpe ratio is meager (0.031).

Summary

- The CAPM metrics, the alpha, and the beta are fascinating to understand the links between the portfolio and the benchmark.

- Drawdown gives us the most significant loss we can have in a period if we enter in position at the worse time of this period.

- Sharpe and Sortino's ratios allow us to understand the return gain for 1% of risk-taking. However, the way to compute the risk is different.

- The VaR and the cVaR allow us to speculate about the worst losses you can have used the strategy.

Chapter 6: Advanced backtest methods

This chapter discusses advanced backtest technic such as take-profit, stop-loss backtest, interesting metrics, and trailing stop loss. It will give us more ideas about measures used in finance and trading.

6.1 Useful backtest advice

We have already seen how to make a backtest, but we have not discussed the most frequent errors among more than 60,000 students.

6.1.1 Backtest is not a searching tool

The first and most important rule to follow is "Backtest is not a searching tool." Marco Lopez de Prado said in one of his books: "Backtesting while researching is like drinking and driving."

We will take a little example of the steps followed by nearly all students to highlight the issue in their process:

1. Find some data, create new features, and split the dataset between a train set and a test set.
2. Create a strategy using only the train set
3. Backtest the strategy on the test
4. Repeat until we find a profitable strategy on the test set

STEP 4 IS WHAT WE MUST AVOID !

Why? Because we will obtain hidden strategy overfitting. Without realizing it, we will use a dataset that is supposed to represent reality as much as possible to develop our strategy. However, in reality, we do not have access to the future price: that is the problem! We will use the future to train our algorithms, so we have very different performances in live trading.

Now, let me show the steps to follow to avoid finding a "lucky" strategy or an overfitted strategy like in our previous example:

1. Find the data, create new features, and split the dataset.
2. Create a strategy and OPTIMIZE it on the train set
3. Backtest the strategy on the test set: keep it if it is good or stop here. Do not change the strategy's parameters; the strategy is not profitable. It does not matter; we will try another one!

We need to understand that the more we touch our test set to adapt the strategy, the more we will have bad performances in the future (in live trading).

6.1.2 Big days are not our friends

Obviously big profit days are our friends, so why does the title section tell the opposite? The second rule to follow when we backtest a strategy is not to consider the big profit.

Indeed, the more the event is uncommon on the backtest, the more the probability of facing it again is low. So, suppose we base the profitability of our strategy on these 2 or 3 big profits. In that case, the probability of being profitable in live trading is very low.

Figure 6.1: Strategy with a poor return's stability

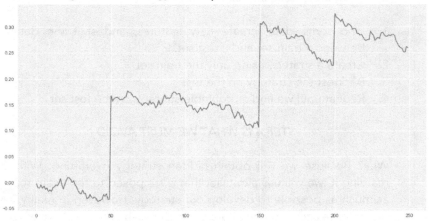

We see that the strategy will be a losing strategy without these three big profits. It means that it is a risky strategy, so, in my opinion, it is better not to select it.

To illustrate this purpose, let us see Figure 6.1 and Figure 6.2, in which we see two strategies with the same return over the period but with very different behavior. The first one loses a significant part of the trades but is good thanks to the three significant earnings. Conversely, the second strategy (Figure 6.2) is much more interesting because the capital growth is more stable.

Figure 6.2: Strategy with an excellent return's stability

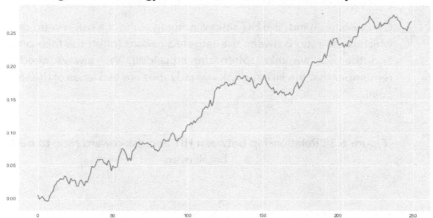

This strategy is much more stable because the profit comes from much of the trade. We do not have big profits or significant losses on the returns, which is essential to see our capital growth safely.

 Never forget that the first goal of trading is to preserve our capital and a second time to make it grow, not the opposite!

6.1.3 Understand your strategy

Doing a backtest is not interesting to predict the future behavior of the strategy returns. The price has followed only one path between an infinite number of possible paths. So, why should we do a backtest? Because it will allow us to understand the strategy's strengths and weaknesses, it is essential before putting it in live trading.

The first thing to check is the HIT ratio, the winning trade percentage: keeping a strategy with a HIT ratio adapted to our goals is essential. For example, suppose we want to create a trading signal to put in copy trading (like in BullTrading). In that case, we should have the highest HIT ratio possible because people will be more confident if they see many profits, even small ones. However, we can accept the lowest HIT ratio if we develop algorithms only for our investment.

On the other hand, the HIT ratio is nothing without a risk-reward ratio, which is the ratio between the targeted reward (often the take-profit) and the risk we take (often the stop-loss). We always need to remember that the HIT and risk-reward ratios are two faces of the same coin!

Figure 6.3 : Relationship between HIT and risk-reward ratio to be at break even

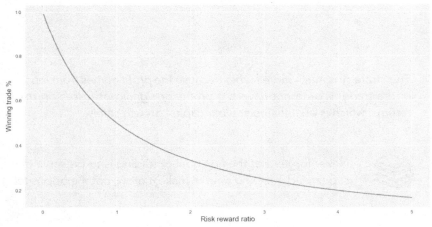

We should find an equilibrium between these two metrics because we will never obtain 95% of the winning trade with R (risk reward ratio) greater than 1. Moreover, it is okay because in Figure 6.3, with a 95% HIT ratio, we only need R of 0.052, which means that if we have a risk of 1%, we need a profit of 0.052% when we earn a trade (with a 95%-win rate) to be at the break-even.

These two metrics are suitable to classify the strategy and understand if they are suitable for our investor profile or not. Moreover, we need to look at more metrics like the trade lifetime and time underwater (when the strategy drawdown is lower than 0, but we will explain it in detail in the next section).

There is no good value for these values; even if the more time underwater is small, the best it is. However, it depends on our strategy target: if we want a scalping strategy. We have a max time underwater of 2 months; it is not good, but if we use a swing strategy, it can be acceptable.

 Always adapt the analysis of your backtest to your target strategy. For example, do not expect a trading lifetime of 10 minutes if you use a swing strategy.

6.2 Compute the strategy returns using TP and SL

This section will show us how to compute the strategy returns using a TP-SL strategy, adapt the data to this backtest method, and analyze the results.

6.2.1 Find the extremum

In the previous chapter, we used vectorized backtesting. However, it is impossible here because we need to check for each position when we have touched the take-profit or the stop-loss. However, if we use the ticks, the backtest will take much time (hours, maybe days if we do not have a performant computer).

So, to fix this issue, we will use a little tip. Indeed, why do we need the ticks? We touch the take-profit or the stop-loss first to find it for each position. So, for each candle, we need to know which came first, the low or the high!

Using only one timeframe will be impossible. However, suppose we use the highest timeframe (ex: hourly) database and the lowest timeframe (ex: 15 min) database. In that case, knowing which is touched first will be possible. The advantage of this strategy is that we keep the same number of data with one new attractive row, which will be called "First" and will tell us if we have touched the high or the low of this candle first. We need to look at the Github repository (link in chapter 1) to find the database used in the code.

Code 6.1: Find if the first touch price: Low or High

```python
def find_timestamp_extremum(data, df_lowest_timeframe):
    """

    :params: data(highest timeframe OHLCV data), df_lowest_timeframe
    (lowest timeframe OHLCV data)
    :return: data with three new columns: Low_time (TimeStamp),
    High_time (TimeStamp), High_first (Boolean)
    """


    # Set new columns
    data["Low_time"] = np.nan
    data["High_time"] = np.nan
    data["First"] = np.nan


    # Loop to find out which of the Take Profit and Stop loss appears
    first
    for i in tqdm(range(len(data) - 1)): 1


        # Extract values from the lowest timeframe dataframe
        start = data.iloc[i:i + 1].index[0]
        end = data.iloc[i + 1:i + 2].index[0]
        row_lowest_timeframe = df_lowest_timeframe.loc[start:end].
        iloc[:-1]


        # Extract Timestamp of the max and min over the period
    (highest timeframe)
        try:
            high = row_lowest_timeframe["high"].idxmax()
            low = row_lowest_timeframe["low"].idxmin()

            data.loc[start, "Low_time"] = low
            data.loc[start, "High_time"] = high


        except Exception as e:
```

```
            print(e)
            data.loc[start, "Low_time"] = start
            data.loc[start, "High_time"] = start

        # Find out which appears first
        data.loc[data["High_time"] > data["Low_time"], "First"] = 1
        data.loc[data["High_time"] < data["Low_time"], "First"] = 2
        data.loc[data["High_time"] == data["Low_time"], "First"] = 0  2


        # Verify the number of row without both TP and SL on same time
        percentage_garbage_row=len(data.loc[data["First"]==0].dropna())
/ len(data) * 100

        #if percentage_garbage_row<95:
        print(f"WARNINGS: Garbage row: {'%.2f' % percentage_garbage_row}
%")  3


        # Transform the columns in datetime columns
        data.High_time = pd.to_datetime(data.High_time)
        data.Low_time = pd.to_datetime(data.Low_time)

        # We delete the last row because we can't find the extremum
        data = data.iloc[:-1]

        # Specific to the current data
        if "timestamp" is data.columns:
            del data["timestamp"]

        return data
```

1   Iterate on each highest timeframe row and select the associated lowest timeframe rows to find the first touch highest timeframe point using the low and high price of the lowest timeframe.

2   Sometimes, you will have some undetermined row if the high and the low of the highest timeframe is a touch on the same lowest timeframe row.

3 Compute the number of rows in which we cannot find which extremum is touched first

We have 0.86% of undetermined rows in our example, so it is acceptable. However, if we have more than 5% of garbage row, it is better to take a lower timeframe.

6.2.2 Calculate the returns

Once we have a complete database with our OHLCV data and we have a new row which tells us which extremum is touched first, we can compute the returns of our strategy using a TP-SL exit strategy.

To put our backtest into practice, we need a signal: -1 if we want to take a sell position, 0 if we hold, and 1 if we take a buy position. However, if we do not have these signals, we can simulate them using the following code.

Code 6.2: Compute random signals

```
# Create random signals
np.random.seed(70)
values = [-1, 0, 1]
df["Signal"] = [np.random.choice(values
              , p=[0.10, 0.80, 0.10]) for _ in range(len(df))]
```

It will be very simple. To compute the returns using a Take-profit / Stop-loss exit strategy, we need to consider four cases:

1. We open a buy position, and we touch the TP first (High price)
2. We open a buy position, and we touch the SL first (Low price)
3. We open a sell position, and we touch the TP first (Low price)
4. We open a sell position, and we touch the SL first (High price)

It is a little bit fastidious, but the reasoning is straightforward: we have a signal, and at the opening of the next candle, we open a trade (buy or sell, depending on it). Then, for each high and low, we check the variation from the open to the current high and low to see if we have crossed or not the TP or the SL.

Code 6.3: Backtest using TP and SL

```
def run_tp_sl(data, leverage=1, tp=0.015, sl=-0.015, cost=0.00):
    """

    :params (mandatory): data(have to contain a High_time and a
Low_time columns)
    :params (optional): leverage=1, tp=0.015, sl=-0.015, cost=0.00
    :return: data with three new columns: Low_time (TimeStamp),
High_time (TimeStamp), High_first (Boolean)
    """


    # Set some parameters
    buy=False
    sell=False
    data["duration"] = 0


    for i in range(len(data)):

        # Extract data
        row = data.iloc[i]


        ######## OPEN BUY ########
        if buy==False and row["Signal"]==1:
            buy = True
            open_buy_price = row["open"]
            open_buy_date = row.name

        #VERIF
        if buy:
            var_buy_high = (row["high"] - open_buy_price) /
            open_buy_price
            var_buy_low = (row["low"] - open_buy_price) /
        open_buy_price

            # VERIF FOR TP AND SL ON THE SAME CANDLE
            if (var_buy_high > tp) and (var_buy_low < sl): 1

                # IF TP / SL ON THE SAME TIMESTAMP, WE DELETE THE
    TRADE RETURN
                if row["Low_time"] == row["High_time"]:
```

```
                pass

        elif row["First"]==2:
            data.loc[row.name, "returns"] = (tp-cost) *
            leverage
            data.loc[row.name, "duration"] = row.High_time —
            open_buy_date

        elif row["First"]==1:
            data.loc[row.name, "returns"] = (sl-cost) *
            leverage
            data.loc[row.name, "duration"] = row.Low_time —
            open_buy_date

        buy = False
        open_buy_price = None
        var_buy_high = 0
        var_buy_low = 0
        open_buy_date = None

    elif var_buy_high > tp:
        data.loc[row.name, "returns"] = (tp-cost) * leverage
        buy = False
        open_buy_price = None
        var_buy_high = 0
        var_buy_low = 0
        data.loc[row.name, "duration"] = row.High_time —
        open_buy_date
        open_buy_date = None

    elif var_buy_low < sl:
        data.loc[row.name, "returns"] = (sl-cost) * leverage
        buy = False
        open_buy_price = None
        var_buy_high = 0
        var_buy_low = 0
        data.loc[row.name, "duration"] = row.Low_time —
        open_buy_date
        open_buy_date = None


######## OPEN SELL ########
if sell==False and row["Signal"]==-1:
```

```python
        sell = True
        open_sell_price = row["open"]
        open_sell_date = row.name

#VERIF
if sell: 2
    var_sell_high = -(row["high"] - open_sell_price) /
    open_sell_price
    var_sell_low = -(row["low"] - open_sell_price) /
    open_sell_price

    if (var_sell_low > tp) and (var_sell_high < sl):

        if row["Low_time"] == row["High_time"]:
            pass
        elif row["First"]==1: #À INVERSER POUR LE BUY
            data.loc[row.name, "returns"] = (tp-cost) *
            leverage
            data.loc[row.name, "duration"] = row.Low_time —
            open_sell_date

        elif row["First"]==2:
            data.loc[row.name, "returns"] = (sl-cost) *
            leverage
            data.loc[row.name, "duration"] = row.High_time —
            open_sell_date

        sell = False
        open_sell_price = None
        var_sell_high = 0
        var_sell_low = 0
        open_sell_date = None

    elif var_sell_low > tp:
        data.loc[row.name, "returns"] = (tp-cost) * leverage
        sell = False
        open_sell_price = None
        var_sell_high = 0
        var_sell_low = 0
        data.loc[row.name, "duration"] = row.Low_time —
        open_sell_date
        open_sell_date = None
```

```
elif var_sell_high < sl:
    data.loc[row.name, "returns"] = (sl-cost) * leverage
    sell = False
    open_sell_price = None
    var_sell_high = 0
    var_sell_low = 0
    data.loc[row.name, "duration"] = row.High_time —
    open_sell_date
    open_sell_date = None


# Put 0 when we have missing values
data["returns"] = data["returns"].fillna(value=0)  3
return data
```

1   We must check first if both TP and SL are crossed in the same row to look at the First columns to see which is touched first (if First = 0, we do not count the trade)

2   We need to be very careful when we compute the selling positions profit because we need to use the low time to find the TP and the high time to find the SL.

3   It would help if we replaced all the Nan values with zeros to compute the backtest metrics efficiently.

We have already made the backtest but do not know how to interpret it. Indeed, we have a return series without clear information. That is the point of the next section

6.2.3 Analyze the backtest

Computing the returns is not enough; we need to calculate different metrics for a quick overview of our strategy performance. To do that, we will change our previous backtest function a little bit.

The most significant modification in the output is that we do not have the Sharpe and Sortino ratio in this backtest. Why? Because the TP and SL are fixed, there is no utility to compute the volatility, especially the downward volatility, because all the losses are equal to the stop-loss minus the fees. So, we can replace that with the average trade lifetime and the VaR over cVaR ratio by the TUW (time underwater) because the ratio will be close to 1 because of the stop-loss.

Figure 6.4: Random signal backtest

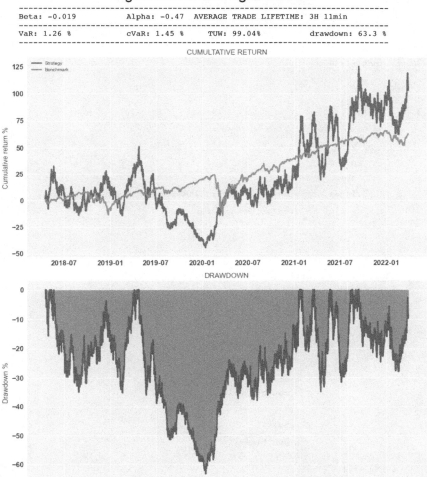

```
--------------------------------------------------------------------
Beta: -0.019        Alpha: -0.47   AVERAGE TRADE LIFETIME: 3H 11min
--------------------------------------------------------------------
VaR: 1.26 %         cVaR: 1.45 %     TUW: 99.04%         drawdown: 63.3 %
--------------------------------------------------------------------
```

Just take one minute to analyze the backtest. Here, the strategy will go directly to the bin. Why? Because of the risk, it takes. The TUW equals 99.04%, with a drawdown max of 63.3%.

Moreover, we can also display the monthly returns, which can be an interesting indication. Let us know how to do it in the following code and see the result in Figure 6.5.

Code 6.4: Compute monthly returns

```
# Bonus
def profitable_month_return(p):
        total = 0
        positif = 0


        r=[]
        # Loop on each different year
        for year in p.index.strftime("%y").unique():
            e = []
            nbm                                              =
    p.loc[p.index.strftime("%y")==year].index.strftime("%m").unique()
            # Loop on each different month
            for mois in nbm:


                monthly_values                               =
    p.loc[p.index.strftime("%y:%m")==f"{year}:{mois}"]
                sum_ = monthly_values.sum()


                # Verifying that there is at least 75% of the values
                if len(monthly_values)>15:


                    # Computing sum return
                    s = monthly_values.sum()


                    if s>0:
                        positif+=1


                    else:
                        pass


                    total+=1


                else:
                    pass
                e.append(sum_)
            r.append(e)
```

```
    r[0]=[0 for _ in range(12-len(r[0]))] + r[0]
    r[-1]= r[-1]  + [0 for _ in range(12-len(r[-1]))]
    return
pd.DataFrame(r,columns=["January","February","March","April","May",
"June",

"July","August","September","October","November","December"],
index=p.index.strftime("%y").unique())


def heatmap(data):
    htm = profitable_month_return(data["returns"])*100
    htm.index.name = "Year"
    htm.index = [f"20{idx}" for idx in htm.index]

    plt.figure(figsize=(20,8))
    pal = sns.color_palette("RdYlGn",n_colors=15)
    sns.heatmap(htm, annot=True, cmap =pal, vmin=-100, vmax=100)

    plt.title("Heatmap Monthly returns")
    plt.show()
```

Figure 6.5: Heatmap monthly returns

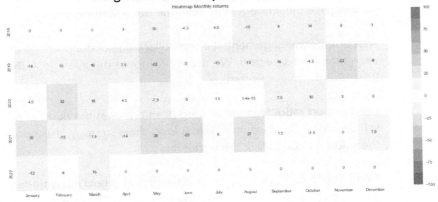

It is a very interesting way to show visually the stability of the strategy performance.

6.3 Advanced backtest tools

Once we have a classic backtest, we can adjust the metrics and simulate different paths. Moreover, we can easily backtest a trailing stop loss strategy.

6.3.1 Backtest metrics list

In this section, we will recap several backtest indicators (some that we have already seen in the book, but we will put them here again to have a complete list of indicators). This is a non-exhaustive list!

1. **Time underwater**: the percentage of time we have a drawdown below 0. It allows us to understand the percentage of time we will earn money. It is essential to understand that the time does not give the intensity of the loss: we can have a 1% time underwater and a max drawdown of 100%, so we will lose all of our capital. This metric should always be combined to the maximum drawdown.

2. **Trade lifetime**: the average time of a trade position. The more scalping-like the strategy, the more the trade lifetime is essential.

3. **Assets under management**: It is the dollar value of our portfolio at each time (it is a vector). We usually compute the average AUM (assets under management).

4. **Long – short ratio**: Number of long positions over the number of sell positions. So, if we work with a long-short strategy, the more the value is close to 0.5, the better it is.

5. **Number of trades**: very important to understand how many trades you take and see if it is accorded to your trading plan: a strategy with 12 trades over a year is not a significative backtest but 500 is.

6. **Annualized returns**: It is essential to compute the annualized return to be able to compare several strategies between them.

7. **Correlation to underlying**: Pearson's correlation is usually between the strategy returns and the underlying returns. The more the

value is close to 1, the more the strategy long the asset and the more the correlation is close to -1, the more the strategy short the asset. So, the strategy is not adding a lot of value if the correlation is close to -1 or 1.

8. **HIT ratio:** percentage of winning trade. It must be associated with the risk-reward ratio.

9. **Risk-reward ratio:** Essential to understand how many our risk is compared to our targeted reward. Again, HIT and risk-reward ratios (R ratios) are the two faces of the same coin

10. **Sharpe ratio:** An essential financial metric, it allows us to understand the benefits of return of one more percentage risk. It must be annualized.

11. **Sortino ratio:** Same metric as the Sharpe ratio, but we compute the risk using the downward volatility instead of the classic volatility for the Sharpe ratio.

12. **Beta:** It will give us some indications about how much the strategy is correlated to the market (SP500, for example) (more explanation in chapter 5)

13. **Alpha:** tells us how the strategy overperforms or underperforms the market. (More explanation in chapter 5)

14. **Information ratio:** it will allow us to compare the risk-reward couple of the strategy to the benchmark risk-reward couple.

15. **Risk-free asset return:** Consider the risk-free asset returns over the period (annualized) to compare them to the annualized strategy returns.

16. **VaR:** Will give us the worst loss we can make with a 5% error threshold. We can compute it on the period that you want: the worst loss per day, month or year for example. (More explanation in chapter 5)

17. **cVaR:** Like the VaR but some difference in the computation. (More explanation in chapter 5)

Use 20 backtest metrics will not render your strategy better. In my opinion, 5 good indicators are clearly enough to have a quick overview.

6.3.2 Monte Carlo simulation

So far, we have analyzed the performance of our strategy on only one possible path. Indeed, the past is only one possible path between an infinity.

To analyze different possible paths, we can use Monte Carlo simulations. To create one Monte-Carlo simulation, we will randomly take the strategy returns and reorganize the data.

Code 6.4: Compute monthly returns

```
def monte_carlo(data, method="simple"): 1
    random_returns = []
    data["returns"] = data["returns"].fillna(value=0)

    for _ in tqdm(range(100)):
        returns = data["returns"]-10**-100 2
        np.random.shuffle(returns)
        random_returns.append(returns)

    if method=="simple":
        df_ret                                                    =
pd.DataFrame(random_returns).transpose().cumsum()*100
        cur_ret = data["returns"].cumsum()*100
    else:
        df_ret                                                    =
((1+pd.DataFrame(random_returns).transpose()).cumprod()-1)*100
        cur_ret = ((1+data["returns"]).cumprod()-1)*100

    p_90 = np.percentile(df_ret, 99, axis=1)
    p_50 = np.percentile(df_ret, 50, axis=1)
    p_10 = np.percentile(df_ret, 1, axis=1)
```

```
plt.figure(figsize=(20,8))

plt.plot(df_ret.index, p_90, color="#39B3C7")
plt.plot(df_ret.index, p_50, color="#39B3C7")
plt.plot(df_ret.index, p_10, color="#39B3C7")

plt.plot(cur_ret,    color="blue",    alpha=0.60,    linewidth=3,
label="Current returns")


plt.fill_between(df_ret.index, p_90, p_10,
                 p_90>p_10,   color="#669FEE",   alpha=0.20,
label="Monte carlo area")


plt.ylabel("Cumulative returns %", size=13)
plt.title("MONTE CARLO SIMULATION", size=20)

plt.legend()
plt.show()
```

1   We can choose the method of capitalization. The results will differ if we use simple or compounded capitalization.

2   For each simulation, we need to change a little bit the values to shuffle the data again (it is just a programming constraint), but it will change nothing to the results.

Once we have several simulations, we need to plot them intelligently. To highlight the different possible paths, we will create a Monte-Carlo area (between the dynamic 1st centile and 99th centile) and put the dynamic median with the returns like in Figure 6.6.

It is essential to do this analysis to understand the loss that we have had in the worst case (1st centile curve). In our case, we can see that we have lost nearly all our capital in the first year. This strategy is too volatile because even if it is followed the strategy distribution, it is possible to have lost 90% of our capital in the first year.

When we have our Monte-Carlo area, the best thing to see is a short area close to an upward trending line. The more area is small, the less the strategy is volatile.

Figure 6.6: Monte-Carlo simulation with simple interest capitalization

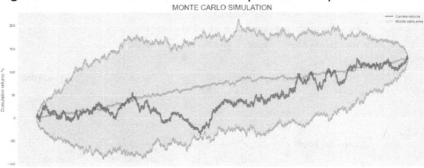

Seen the lower band of the Monte-Carlo, we can see that in one of the worst paths, we can lose a lot of many after our strategy launching. Moreover, the Monte-Carlo area is too large.

6.3.3 Easy Trailing stop

Trailing stop loss required ticks to be computed correctly. However, here is a quick tip for finding the worst-case possible using a trailing stop loss strategy. So, if we use the backtest function that will find the worst case, we will see if, in the worst case, we are profitable or not. If yes, it is a good thing because it means that all the big profits from the trailing stop loss will be a bonus.

There are a lot of other trailing stop losses like classic trailing stop loss and double profit targets. In our example, we will use the threshold trailing stop loss. Once we have touched the TP, we begin the Trailing Stop Loss (TSL) with a margin of 0.1%. It means that when we touch the TP, we secure 1.4% with a TP of 1.5%, and then we use a classic TSL: for each price augmentation, we increase the stop loss to secure more and more profit. The goal will be to find the returns. If we never earn any bonus profit from the trailing stop loss, check the strategy's profitability to increase the probability of profitability in live trading.

Code 6.5: Compute monthly returns

```
def run_tsl(data, leverage=1, tp=0.015, sl=-0.015, tsl= 0.001, cost=0.00):
    """

    :params (mandatory): data(have to contain a High_time and a Low_time
columns)
    :params (optional): leverage=1, tp=0.015, sl=-0.015, cost=0.00
    :return: data with three new columns: Low_time (TimeStamp), High_time
(TimeStamp), High_first (Boolean)
    """

    tpl = tp - tsl 1
```

1   The only difference with the run_tpsl function is that we need to
have the TSL margin.

Sometimes compute the worst case of a strategy or an indicator is much easier to compute the whole process. Use it in your advantage.

As shown in figure 6.7, the random signal with worst-case TSL is not profitable. This is because of poor strategy robustness with high volatility underlying.

Logically, the worst TSL case is not very good. However, the goal will be too delicate, something with acceptable returns, which will increase the probability of being profitable in the future. It will be much more difficult in creation but much easier when we are in live trading, and we need to know when we want to suffer.

Figure 6.7: Worst TSL case with a random signal

| Beta: -0.018 | Alpha: -3.13 % | AVERAGE TRADE LIFETIME: 3H 11min |
| VaR: 1.32 % | cVaR: 1.5 % | TUW: 99.71% | drawdown: 87.8 % |

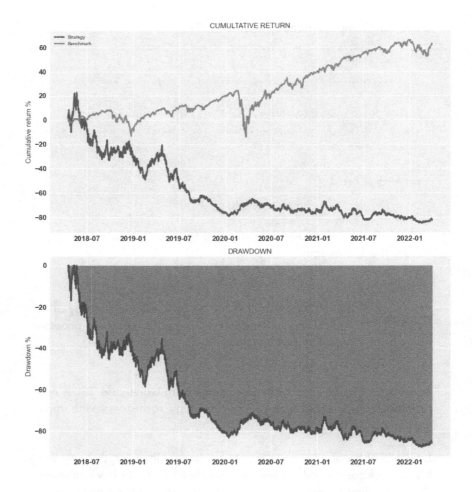

Summary

- Understand how to process to create a Backtest as clean as possible.

- How to create a long-short backtest using TP and SL as exit signals.

- There are many metrics to understand our backtest (17 in the chapter but an infinity that can be used). Do not forget that making 20 backtest metrics will not render our strategy better!

- Use Monte-Carlo simulation to understand different previous possible paths of your data

- How to compute an easy Trailing Stop Loss

Part 2: Statistics predictive models

This part discusses the classic technique used in the financial industry. First, we will learn the statistical arbitrage trading with an example: pair trading. Then we will talk about the ARMA model to predict the returns of stocks. And to finish, we will see more profound the notion of linear regression and the classification concept with the logistic regression.

Summary:

Chapter 7: Statistical Arbitrage Trading

Chapter 8: Auto Regressive Moving Average (ARMA) models

Chapter 9: Linear regression and Logistic regression

Chapter 7: Statistical arbitrage Trading

In this chapter, we will discuss statistical arbitrage in finance. The notion will be learned through the pair trading strategy. First, we will see the idea of stationarity and cointegration. Then, we will explain how the pairs trading strategy works.

Before we begin the chapter, let us talk about statistical arbitrage. This chapter will only see one of many examples of the statistical arbitrage strategy.

Theoretically, making a long-term profit with a trading strategy is impossible because the market should be equilibrium and efficient. However, in reality, it is a little bit different. Indeed, there are many unbalances in the financial market, and the statistical arbitrage strategies make this disequilibrium in a profit. For example, one of the most straightforward strategies is to find errors in the Forex quotations.

For example, we have the following pairs of currencies: NZD/AUD=1, AUD/CAD=1.5, and NZD/CAD=1. If we have CAD and want to use a statical arbitrage opportunity to make a profit. Using the third pair of currency, we can buy 100NZD because 100NZD=100AUD and 100AUD=150CAD. It is a statistical opportunity trading because we have 100CAD. We can have 150CAD using an **imbalance** in the market with no risk.

7.1. Stationarity to Cointegration

This section will study the stationarity of a time series and how to use the stationarity of time series to find cointegration between two time series.

7.1.1. Stationarity

The stationarity of a time series is essential because it is a crucial point of the behavior of a time series.

There is stationarity if the time series is **flat around the mean and without trend**. Moreover, it needs to have a **constant variance in time**.[7] (There are many assumptions to check, but these are the most important).

A time series tends to return to a constant mean if it is stationary. So, it is a good thing if you want to use statistical arbitrage trading.

We can check the stationarity of a time series using the Dick and Fuller test. The test's null hypothesis (H0) is that the time series is not stationary. So, suppose we have a p-value inferior at error threshold s. In that case, hypothesis H0 is not accepted, and it is a stationarity time series. For example, if we want to know at an error threshold of 10% (if the time series is stationary), we will compute an augmented Dick and Fuller test and check if the p-value is below or above 10%. So, there are the following possibilities:

- **p > 0.10**: H0 is accepted, and the time series is not stationary. We need to make some modifications if we want it to become stationary.

- **p < 0.10**: H0 is not accepted, and the time series is stationary.

There are many tests to determine whether a time series is stationary. However, be careful because all tests have different null hypotheses, for one is stationarity, and the other is non-stationarity.

---

[7] **Additional lecture:** Stationarity and differencing

Here are some pictures of stationarity and non-stationarity time series. In figure 7.1 and figure 7.2, we can see a non-stationary and stationary time series, respectively.

Figure 7.1: Non-stationary series

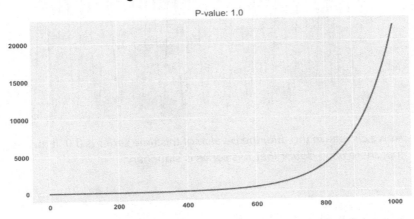

As we can see in the title, the p-value of this time series is 1.0. It means that there is no doubt that this series is not stationary.

 The more the p-value is close to 0, the higher the chance the time series is stationary.

On the next page, Figure 7.2 shows the behavior of a stationary time series. It is the most stationarity data that we can have. So, we can find the differences between figure 7.1 and figure 7.2.

Figure 7.2: Stationary time series

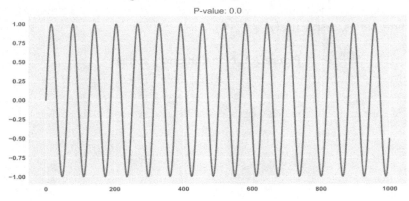

As we can see in the title, the p-value of this time series is 0.0. It means that there is no doubt that this series is stationary.

7.1.2. Cointegration

Many of the time, the stock prices are not stationary. So, how can we apply models which need stationary data? To do it, we are going to talk about cointegration. **The cointegration allows us to find a stationary time series combining non-stationaries time series.**[8]

 To find if two time series are cointegrated, you need to find a relationship like this (where Y and X are two time series) $Y = \alpha + \beta * X + \varepsilon$, where ε **is stationary** (the error term) and X and Y are two **non-stationary** time series.

So, to create a cointegration test, we need to compute linear regression. We will learn how it works in detail in one of the following chapters. Now, the only thing we need to know is that the purpose of the regression is to find relations between the data. As we have seen before in the tips box, the linear regression gives us the alpha and the beta to approximate the Y, only knowing the X and the epsilon is the error term.

---

[8] **Additional lecture** : Cointegration, Niti Gupta

Code 7.1: cointegration test

```
import statsmodels.api as stat
import statsmodels.tsa.stattools as ts

def cointegration(x, y):
    ols = stat.OLS(x, y).fit() 1
    adf_results = ts.adfuller(ols.resid) 2
    if adf_results[1] <= 0.1: 3
        return 'Cointegration'
    else:
        return 'No Cointegration'
```

1   Fit linear regression using Statsmodels.

2   *ols.resid* allows us to take the residuals easily.

3   The threshold for the acceptability of the test is 0.1. It means 10%.

 With Python, it is easier to work with the best library for each situation. **StatsModels** is better when you need to do statistics tasks with linear regression, and if you want to do a linear regression for machine learning, you will use **Scikit-learn**.

Figure 7.3 shows the difference between two cointegrated time series. Indeed, in the figure, we can see the residual between both time series. In this example, both the series are not stationary. Indeed, the p-value for the augmented dick fuller test for the two times series equals 1. Moreover, the p-value of the augmented dick and fuller test for the residuals are 0. So, the residuals are stationary. Moreover, it is possible to see that in the figure without computations.

Figure 7.3: Cointegrate two time series

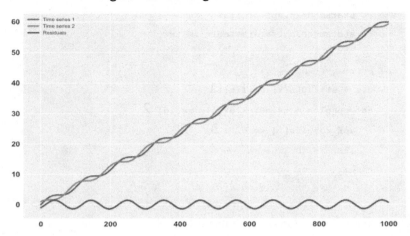

As we can see, the residuals of this times series are stationary, and this implies that the two series are cointegrated because it is also easy to see that the two time series are not stationary.

7.2. Pairs trading

In the previous section, we have seen some statistics notions. In this section, we will apply them to a financial context with a pairs trading strategy[9].

7.2.1. How it works

In this part, we will talk about how pairs trading works theoretically. It will allow us to understand how to choose the best assets and process to do this strategy:

- **We need to execute a qualitative analysis of the two pairs**: we need assets of the same sector. For example, BTC/USD and ETH/USD. Then, it is less critical, but we need to find assets

---

[9] **Additional lecture**: Pairs Trading, James Chen

with similar market capitalization and equivalent daily traded volumes.

- **We analyze if the time series are cointegrated**: this is the essential part of the process. We need to have two non-stationary time series with stationary residuals to find a linear relationship between the two assets.

- **Analyze the correlation**: if we have a set of assets and too many with cointegration, we can take the n best-correlated asset (in returns).

Once we have done this, we have the pair of assets to do the pair trading strategy. It is necessary to compute z-scores using the differences between the two time series for the dynamic portfolio (if you do not remember how to do that, you can go to section 4.1).

 For the pair trading strategy, you can compute the z-score using the difference of log difference. It is a personal choice.

Now that we have the z-score, we need to define the long and short signals. There are many ways to do it. One of these ways is to enter positions when we pass a standard deviation threshold and exit the positions at the mean of the spread.

Figure 7.4 shows the spread of figure 7.3 with the standard deviation and the mean of the values. The green circle represents a short position for time series 1 and a long position for time series 2. Indeed, the spread is ts1 minus ts2. We need a decrease of the time series 1 or an increase of the time series 2, to return to the mean of the spread. The red circle represents the inverse for the positions because the spread is negative.

Figure 7.4: Spread with thresholds

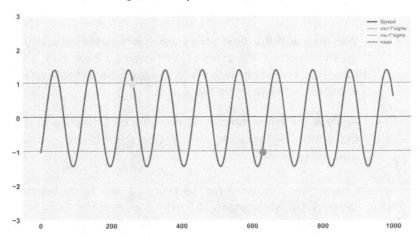

This figure shows the spread with the standard deviation and means of the spread and the enter position signal.

It is essential to enter in position when the spread crosses the threshold a second time and not before because the spread can continue to increase the first time.

7.2.2. Applications

In this part, we are going to compute a pair trading strategy. First, we will use a function to find the cointegrate pairs and the correlation between the two assets to choose the better pair.

We have a list of 10 currencies, and we need to find all combinations of 2 currencies of these ten currencies. To find the number of combinations, we can use the following formula:

$$C_r^n = \frac{n!}{r!\,(n-r)!}$$

Where n is the number of the elements and r the number of elements we choose by combination. Here $r=2$ and $n = 10$ because for each combination we choose 2 assets in the 10.

 n! is the product of all numbers from 1 to n. For example, $10! = 1 * 2 * 3 * 4 * 5 * 6 * 7 * 8 * 9 * 10$. It is called the factorial.

Once we know that we will have 45 possible combinations, we compute them in a list with the code 7.2.

Code 7.2: Find the combinations

```
# We need to find the number of combinations of 2 by 10

# 10! / (2!*8!) = 45 1


# Initialize the variables

nbc = 0

list_com = []


while nbc <45:
    # Take the assetes for the pair randomly
    c1 = np.random.choice(currencies)
    c2 = np.random.choice(currencies) 2


    # Add the list of the two asset
    if c1 != c2 and [c1, c2] not in list_com and [c2, c1] not in
list_com:
        list_com.append([c1,c2])
        nbc+=1 3
```

1   We can compute the factorial using *np.math.factorial(n)*.

2   *np.random.choice()* takes a value of the list randomly.

3   Add 1 to the number of pairs to stop the loop when nbc=45.

We verify if [c1,c2] and [c2,c1] is not in the list of the combinations because it is the same pair. Example: (EUR/USD, USD/AUD) = (USD/AUD, EUR/USD).

Now, we have the possible combination. We need to compute the cointegration and the correlation between the two assets of each pair. We will use the previous cointegration function to do it. We can see in code 7.3 how to compute these metrics efficiently for each pair.

Code 7.3: Compute the correlation and the cointegration test

```
# Initialize the storage variable for all row
resume = []
for com in list_com:
  # Initialize the list
  row = []

  # Add the name of the assets in the list
  row.extend(com)

  # Add the result of the cointegration test
  row.append(cointegration(train_set[com[0]].values,
train_set[com[1]].values))

  # Add the results of the correlation
  row.append(train_set[com].pct_change(1).corr().values[0][1])

  # Add each row to make a list of lists
  resume.append(row)

# Create a dataframe to a better visualization
sum = pd.DataFrame(resume,columns=["Asset1", "Asset2",
    "Cointegration", "Cor"])

# Filtered the row by the cointegred pair
sum.loc[sum["Cointegration"] == "Cointegration"]
```

We will use the list of list structure because it does not depend on the number of pairs. So, we can apply this code to any list of pairs.

Figure 7.5: Resume of the metrics for each pair

Asset 1	Asset 2	Cointegration	Correlation
NZDUSD	AUDNZD	True	-0.27
AUDNZD	EURUSD	True	-0.01
USDCHF	EURUSD	True	-0.55
EURAUD	USDCHF	True	-0.15

In this figure, we can see the cointegrated pairs of the 45 possible combinations.

Instinctively, the lower the negative correlation between the asset's return, the better the strategy will work because we take inverse positions. Whereas (USDCHF, EURUSD) and (NZDUSD, AUDZND) take no positions with this strategy (you can verify with the code). So, we take the pair (EURAUD, USDCHF). We can see the result of the strategy in figure 7.6.

Figure 7.6: Performance of the strategy on (EUR/AUD,USD/CHF

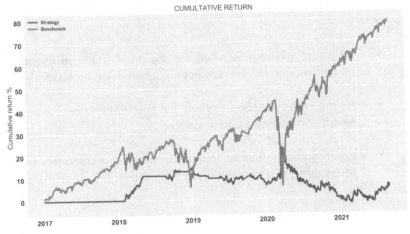

Beta: -0.016   Alpha: 1.41 %.   Sharpe: 0.047.   Sortino: 0.056

VaR: 17.6 %.   cVaR: 20.01 %.   VaR/cVaR: 1.137.   drawdown:24.86 %

121

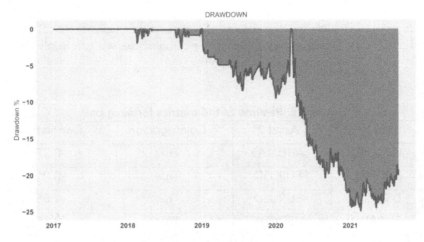

This figure shows the backtest of the pairs trading strategy on EURAUD USDCHF. The backtest is not exciting because the cumulative returns are not very high. We have a little Sharpe ratio; above all, the drawdown does not stop growth for 3 years.

The pair trading has a big assumption which is the fact that the market situation must not change. However, the corona crisis has caused a considerable market disequilibrium, and it has not returned to equilibrium quickly.

Summary

- Statistical arbitrage is when we can profit from the financial market with no risk because of an unbalancing in the market.

- A time series is stationary when flat around the mean, without trend, and constant time variance.

- Cointegration is helpful in finance to create a stationary time series using two non-stationary time series.

Application Live Trading and Screener
This code is based on the class created in the annex: MetaTrader

Code 7.7: Application Trading / Screener for Pair trading

```python
import warnings
warnings.filterwarnings("ignore")
from MT5 import *
import numpy as np
import time


def pair_trading(ts1_symbol, ts2_symbol, pair=1):

    mt5.initialize()


    #Import the data
    ts1_data = MT5.get_data(ts1_symbol, 3500)["close"]
    ts2_data = MT5.get_data(ts2_symbol, 3500)["close"]
    train_set = pd.concat((ts1_data, ts2_data), axis=1).dropna()
    train_set.columns = [ts1_symbol, ts2_symbol]


    train_set["spread"] = train_set[ts1_symbol]-train_set[ts2_symbol]


    train_set["z-score"] = (train_set["spread"] -
train_set["spread"].mean()) / train_set["spread"].std()


    std_high = train_set["z-score"].mean() + train_set["z-score"].std()
    std_low = train_set["z-score"].mean() - train_set["z-score"].std()
    mean = train_set["z-score"].mean()


    # Yersteday
    yts1 = train_set[ts1_symbol].values[-2]
    yts2 = train_set[ts2_symbol].values[-2]


    #Today
    pts1 = train_set[ts1_symbol].values[-1]
    pts2 = train_set[ts2_symbol].values[-1]



    # Today data
```

```
    spread = pts1 - pts2
    zscore = (spread-train_set["spread"].mean())/train_set["spread"]
.std()


    # Yersteday
    yspread = yts1 - yts2
    yzscore = (yspread-train_set["spread"].mean())/train_set["spread"]
.std()



    # TS1
    short_ts1 = False
    long_ts1 = False


    if zscore < std_high and yzscore > std_high:
        short_ts1 = True
        long_ts1 = False


    elif zscore > std_low and yzscore < std_low:
        short_ts1 = False
        long_ts1 = True


    else:
        pass

    #TS2
    short_ts2 = False
    long_ts2 = False


    if zscore < std_high and yzscore > std_high:
        short_ts2 = False
        long_ts2 = True


    elif zscore > std_low and yzscore < std_low:
        short_ts2 = True
        long_ts2 = False


    else:
```

```python
        pass


    # Positions
    if pair == 1:

        buy, sell = long_ts1, short_ts1


    else:
        buy, sell = long_ts2, short_ts2


    return buy, sell


# True = Live Trading and False = Screener
live = True



if live:
    current_account_info = mt5.account_info()
    print("--------------------------------------------------------------")
    print("Date: ", datetime.now().strftime("%Y-%m-%d %H:%M:%S"))
    print(f"Balance: {current_account_info.balance} USD, \t"
          f"Equity: {current_account_info.equity} USD, \t"
          f"Profit: {current_account_info.profit} USD")
    print("--------------------------------------------------------------")



# Initialize the inputs
symbols = ["EURUSD", "EURGBP"]
lots = [0.01, 0.01]
pairs = [1,2]



start = datetime.now().strftime("%H:%M:%S") #"23:59:59"
while True:
    # Verfication for launch
    if datetime.now().weekday() not in (5,1):
        is_time = datetime.now().strftime("%H:%M:%S") == start
    else:
        is_time = False
```

125

```python
# Launch the algorithm
if is_time:

    for symbol, lot, pair in zip(symbols, lots, pairs):


        # Create the signals
        buy, sell = pair_trading(symbols[0], symbols[1], pair=pair)


        # Run the algorithm
        if live:

            MT5.run(symbol, buy, sell,lot)


        else:

            print(f"Symbol: {symbol}\t"
                  f"Buy: {buy}\t"
                  f"Sell: {sell}")
    time.sleep(1)
```

The live parameter sets the live trading mode (live = True) or the screener mode (live = False).

Chapter 8: Auto Regressive Moving Average model (ARMA)

In this chapter, we will explain how works the ARMAs models. In the first section, we will explore the time series concepts. Then, we will explain the AR model and the MA model. Moreover, we will explain the ARMA model and its derivatives.

8.1. Time series basics

This section explains some prerequisites of the time series[10] concept. We will explain the idea of trends, cycles, and seasonality. Then, we will explain some interesting things about the different ways to compute the returns. After that, we will explain the easier to understand predictive model: the linear regression.

8.1.1. Trend, cycle, seasonality

Time series has three essential concepts: trend, cycle, and seasonality. Let us start with the easiest. The trend is a long-term behavior followed by the time series. We can see an example in figure 8.1.

Figure 8.1: Upward trend on the stock price Google (2007 to 2021)

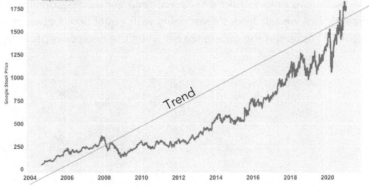

---

[10] **Additional lecture:** What Is a Time Series? Adam Hayes

This figure shows an exponential upward trend for Google stock price from 2007 to 2021. Indeed, we can see that the stock price increases even if there is some downward period.

There is also the possibility of a downward trend in a stock price, but it is only interesting if we can short the stock.

Now, let us talk about the cycle in time series. To explain this, we will create a fictive time series to highlight some points. A time series is cyclical if there is a repeated schema on the price with a non-determined time between two repetitions of this behavior. Let us see an example in figure 8.2.

Figure 8.2: Cyclical time series

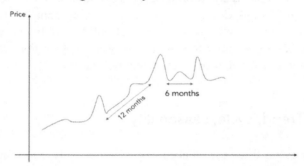

We see that the same behavior sometimes appends but with a non-determinate time between each repetition.

Now, let us see how to find a seasonal time series. Seasonality is like cyclicality, but we talk about seasonality with equal time between each repetition. Let us see the difference between the two concepts in figure 8.3.

Figure 8.3: Seasonal time series

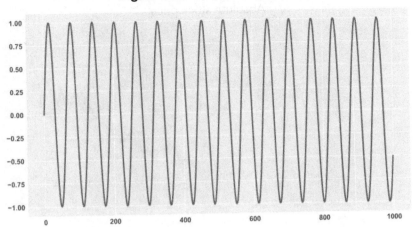

In this figure, we can see the same time between two repetitions of the behavior. So, it is a seasonal time series.

8.1.2. Log price properties

Before going deeper, we need to learn some log price properties. We sometimes use the log price because it allows us to understand the return variation better. Suppose we want to find the best rentability period (for Google stock). In that case, we will check the price of Google and try to see the best augmentation on a graphic. However, the price of a stock is an absolute value, and it does not highlight the relative evolution of the stock. Let us explain this with an example in figure 8.4.

The choice between returns and log returns is a personal choice, but I nearly always test both to optimize my algorithms.

129

Figure 8.4: Log price and price for Google's stock price
Absolute stock price

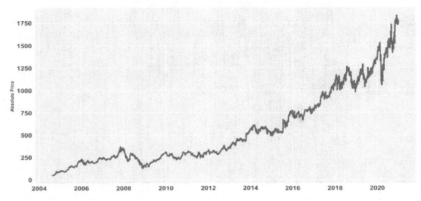

Log stock price

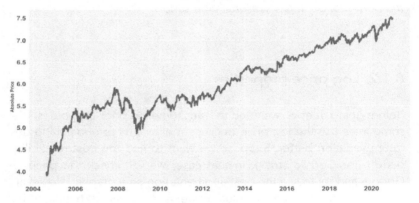

This figure shows that the period from 2005 to 2008 is better than the period from 2017 to 2020 for a long-only strategy thanks to the log price graphic because it puts the price in a minimal range.

8.1.3. The linear regression

In this subsection, we will create a linear regression model. We will explain how linear regression works because this concept is necessary to understand the ARMAs models.

Linear regression is a predictive algorithm. The goal of this algorithm is to allow us to predict some data. For example, suppose we know the relationship between gold and S&P 500. We can use linear regression to predict the S&P 500 stock price using the gold price.

Let us see how to compute a linear regression using an optimization problem and explain more profoundly the intuition using figure 8.5.

$$min_\beta \sum (\tilde{y}_i - y_i)^2$$

Where $\tilde{y}_i$ is the predicted value, y_i the real value and β are the parameters of the model.

 The intuition of the linear regression can be resumed by an algorithm that tries to find the best way to minimize the distance between the predicted and real values.

Figure 8.5: Linear regression intuition

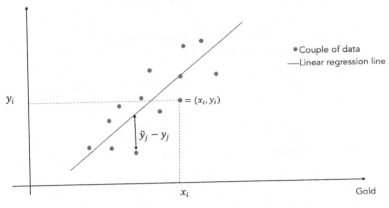

This figure shows how linear regression works with a model that takes the gold and predicts the S&P 500 price.

It is important to understand that for a dataset X which has m rows and n columns $\tilde{y}_i = \beta_0 + \beta_1 x_{i,1} + \cdots + \beta_n x_{i,n}$. In our example with S&P 500 and gold $\tilde{y}_i = \beta_0 + \beta_1\ gold\ price_i$ (β_0 to β_n are the model's parameters).

131

8.2. AR and MA models

In this section, we will learn two practical predictive algorithms: the autoregressive model (AR) and the moving average model (MA).

8.2.1. Autoregressive model (AR)

The intuition behind the autoregressive model is straightforward. It is a linear regression but uses the previous value of the stock to predict the value of today or tomorrow.

For example, if we take the model with S&P 500 and gold again, we predict S&P 500 using gold in the linear regression. Now, we will predict the S&P 500 at time t using S&P 500 at time t-1, which can be extended to S&P 500 at time t-p. Let us see the AR(p) model equation, where p is the number of previous data you take.

$$AR(1): SP500_t = \emptyset_0 + \emptyset_1 SP500_{t-1}$$

$$AR(p): SP500_t = \emptyset_0 + \emptyset_1 SP500_{t-1} + \cdots + \emptyset_p SP500_{t-p}$$

Where $\emptyset_0$ to $\emptyset_p$ are the parameters of the model and each parameter must be a value between 0 and 1.

Now let us see how to do an AR model using Python on the EURUSD currency.

Code 8.1: Implementation AR model

```
def AR_predict_value(train_set):

    """ Function for predict the value of tomorrow using AR model"""

    # Define model
    p = 1
    model = ARIMA(train_set, order=(p, 0, 0))

    # Fit the model
    model_fit = model.fit(disp=0)
```

```
    # Make forecast
    forecast = model_fit.forecast() 1


    return forecast[0][0]
def AR(df,returns=True):
    """ Function to predict the test set with a AR model """

    # Find the split
    split = int(len(df)*0.70)


    # Predict the price using AR function
    df['predicted_value'] = df['Adj Close'].rolling(split).\
apply(AR_predict_value) 2


    # Compute the returns and the signal of the asset
    if returns:
        df['returns'] = df['Adj Close'] 3
        df['signal'] = np.where(df.predicted_value > 0, 1, -1) 4
    else:
        df['returns'] = df['Adj Close'].pct_change(1) 5
        df['signal']   =   np.where(df.predicted_value  >   df['Adj
Close'], 1, -1) 6
    # compute strategy returns
    df['strategy'] = df.signal.shift(1) * df.returns 7


    return df
```

1   Forecast the next value using the fitted model.

2   Apply a function to the whole dataset using *rolling()* from pandas.

3   If we use the returns to fit the model, the columns "returns" is equal to the columns "Adj Close".

4   If the predicted return is positive, we long, and if it is negative, we short.

5   Compute the percentage of return of the asset because "Adj Close" is the absolute price.

6   Create the signal using the condition: if the predicted value is below the Adjusted close, tomorrow we long neither we short.

7   Compute the strategy returns as the signal of yesterday times the returns.

 In the AR function, we have had a parameter return=True. This allows us to work with stock returns or stock prices.

We can answer why doing an AR model with the returns is better than the price. The answer needs some skills from the previous chapter. Indeed, it is better to work with stock return than stock price because we need stationary data (confer section 7.1).

Usually, with AR or ARMA model, we use the differencing methods to transform the data (pt - pt-1). Still, it is difficult for us to use this data because, in finance, we do not just want to predict a value, we want to create a strategy with this value, and we need the percentage of variation to compute the strategy returns. It can be fastidious about calculating returns using different steps while a function exists to do it more accessible.

 In finance, it is better to use returns to have stationary data because it will be easier to compute the returns of the strategy and to compare the assets to each other.

In code 8.1, we can see that the p of the AR model is set to 1 (number of lags for the autoregressive model). But why not 3, 8, or 10? There exist many ways to find the best value for p. The first is to try the model's error using MSE or MAE (confer section 1.1) for p from 1 to 15, for example, and choose the lowest error. However, it can be very long to compute all the models.

The other way is to use a partial autocorrelation graph to find the best theoretical number of lags. Nevertheless, what is partial autocorrelation? A partial autocorrelation summarizes the relationship between an observation in a time series with previous observations with the relationships of intervening observations removed.

Let us see how to interpret a partial autocorrelation graph (you can find the code to do it in the notebook associated with the chapter) in figure 8.6.

Figure 8.6: Partial autocorrelation graph

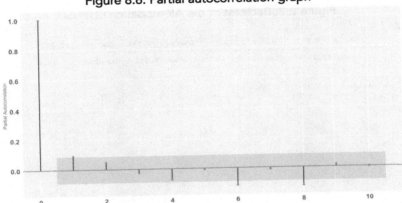

We see the autocorrelation graph of the EURUSD returns. The blue area is the interval in which the partial autocorrelation is not significant, which means that all the lag greater or lower than the blue is significant. Thus, we can see that lag 1, 6, and 8 are significant and have better results. We must choose an AR(8) to estimate the EURUSD model theoretically.

In finance, we always lag slightly to avoid overfitting the algorithm. A maximal lag of 3 can be a good idea because if we take several lags, for example, 150, the model will be perfect on the train data and not useable on the test set. We need a model to predict the value of a test set.

Now, let us talk about the strategy's performance with the AR model. In figure 8.7, we can see the cumulative returns of a method using the AR model on EURUSD. We could say that the model works well enough because, in 1 year, it have made 8% of return even if it had a high risk but, it is not the point highlighted here.

During the corona crisis, the market situation was different from normal. Whereas the AR model is a predictive algorithm that uses past data to predict the value (regressor algorithm), the training data can have very different properties like two other time series.

Figure 8.7: Backtest of the AR model on EURUSD

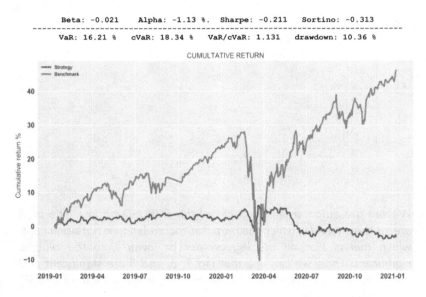

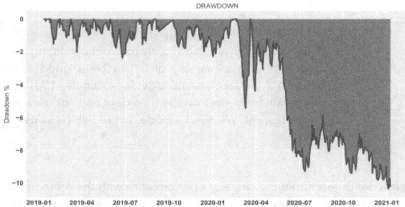

The figure shows that the backtest of the strategy is not good. Indeed, alpha, Sharpe, and Sortino are negative. In contrast, we see an

excellent capacity to predict the return before the corona crisis, even if it is not excellent. Since the corona crisis, the drawdown has had constant growth. Thus, the strategy is not good, and we do not use it like this. We need to search for another asset with a higher partial autocorrelation.

8.2.2. Moving average model (MA)

Now let us talk about the moving average model. This model will not use the moving average as the name but the past error of the model. It is an essential part of the ARMA model because it allows us to learn not from the value of the train set but from the algorithm's error. Let us see how the MA model works with his equation:

$$MA(1): SP500_t = \theta_0 + \theta_1 \varepsilon_{t-1}$$

$$MA(q): SP500_t = \theta_0 + \theta_1 \varepsilon_{t-1} + \cdots + \theta_q \varepsilon_{t-q}$$

Where θ_0 to θ_q are the parameters of the models and $\varepsilon_i = y\,real_i - y\,predict_i$.

Code 8.2: Moving average implementation (MA)

```
def MA_predict_value(train_set):
        """ Function for predict the value of tomorrow using AR model"""

        # Define model
        q = 1
        model = ARIMA(train_set, order=(0, 0, q)) 1

        # Fit the model
        model_fit = model.fit(disp=0)

        # Make forecast
        forecast = model_fit.forecast()

        return forecast[0][0]


    def MA(df,returns=True):
```

```
""" Function to predict the test set with a MA model """


# Find the split
split = int(len(df)*0.70)


# Predict the price using AR function
df['predicted_value'] = df['Adj Close'].rolling(split).\
apply(MA_predict_value)


# Compute the returns of the asset
if returns:
    df['returns'] = df['Adj Close']
    df['signal'] = np.where(df.predicted_value > 0, 1, -1)
else:
    df['returns'] = df['Adj Close'].pct_change(1)
    df['signal']  =  np.where(df.predicted_value  >  df['Adj
Close'], 1, -1)


df['strategy'] = df.signal.shift(1) * df.returns


return df
```

1   The only difference between the AR and the MA models is the parameters of the ARIMA function of StatModels.

 To compute the moving average model (MA), we have used the same function as the AR model, the ARIMA function of statsmodels. Still, there is function parameter difference so this function will be much better explained in the next section.

How to choose the q? We can also use the technique which tests all the q from 1 to 20 to see which has the lowest error on the train set. Alternatively, we can choose the same method as partial autocorrelation but using absolute autocorrelation. Let us see the autocorrelation graph of the EURUSD returns in figure 8.8.

Figure 8.8: Autocorrelation graph for the EURUSD returns

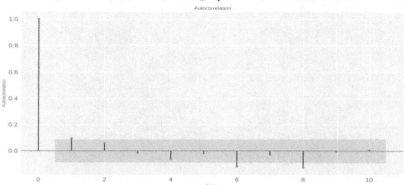

We see that the autocorrelation is insignificant from lag 1 to lag 10 except for lag 6 and 8, but it is tiny.

We choose to take a lag of 1 for this model because there is no autocorrelation. In figure 8.9, we can see the return of the MA(1), which is very similar to the AR(1). However, there is a loss lowest than the AR(1) during the corona crisis because yesterday's error fits it.

When there is no significant partial autocorrelation or autocorrelation, it is advised not to use an AR or MA model. Indeed, sometimes doing nothing is the best action.

Figure 8.9: Backtest MA model on EURUSD

```
Beta: -0.017.  Alpha: 0.68 %   Sharpe: 0.167   Sortino: 0.259
-------------------------------------------------------------------
VaR: 13.76 %   cVaR: 15.92 %   VaR/cVaR: 1.157   drawdown: 8.01 %
```

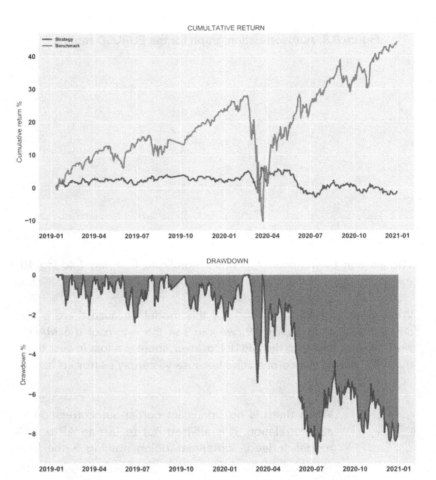

The alpha, Sharpe, and Sortino ratios are positive. However, as for the previous strategy, the strategy does not work anymore after the corona crisis. The excellent point is that the cVaR is equal to 16%, so we should not lose more than 16% in one year.

8.3. ARMAs models

This section will explain the ARMA[11] model, which combines MA and AR models. Then, we answer one of the biggest problems with the ARMA model: how to use an ARMA model on non-stationary data?

---

[11] **Additional lecture:** Autoregressive–moving-average model, Wikipedia

8.3.1. ARMA model

We will explain the autoregressive moving average (ARMA) model in this part. This model is a combination of the AR model and the MA model shown before.

The model is the combination of the AR equation and MA equation. We are going to show the ARMA model equation.
So, an ARMA model has two parameters, q and p. The parameter q is the number of lags for the moving average part, and p is for the autoregressive part.

$$ARMA(1,1):\ y_t = \emptyset_0 + \theta_0 + \emptyset_1 y_{t-1} + \theta_1 \varepsilon_{t-1}$$

$$ARMA(p,q):\ y_t = \emptyset_0 + \theta_0 + \emptyset_1 y_{t-1} + \theta_1 \varepsilon_{t-1} + \cdots + \emptyset_p y_{t-p} + \theta_q \varepsilon_{t-q}$$

Where θ_0 to θ_q are the parameters of the MA part and $\varepsilon_i = y\ real_i - y\ predict_i$, $\emptyset_0$ to $\emptyset_p$ are the parameters of the AR part and each parameter must be a value between 0 and 1.

Remember that the data need to be stationary while using an ARMA model.

Code 8.4: ARMA model implementation

```
def ARMA_predict_value(train_set):

    """ Function for predict the value of tomorrow using AR model"""


    # Define model

    p = 1

    q = 1

    model = ARIMA(train_set, order=(p, 0, q)) 1


    # Fit the model

    model_fit = model.fit(disp=0)


    # Make forecast

    forecast = model_fit.forecast()
```

```
        return forecast[0][0]



def ARMA(df,returns=True):
    """ Function to predict the test set with a ARMA model """

    # Find the split
    split = int(len(df)*0.70)

    # Predict the price using AR function
    df['predicted_value'] = df['Adj Close'].rolling(split).\
apply(ARMA_predict_value)

    # Shift the predicted price by 1 period
    df['predicted_value'] = df['predicted_value'].shift(1)

    # Compute the returns of the asset
    if returns:
        df['returns'] = df['Adj Close']
        df['signal'] = np.where(df.predicted_value > 0, 1, -1)
    else:
        df['returns'] = df['Adj Close'].pct_change(1)
        df['signal']  =  np.where(df.predicted_value  >  df['Adj
Close'], 1, -1)

    df['strategy'] = df.signal.shift(1) * df.returns

    return df
```

1   The only difference between the previous models is the parameters of the ARIMA function of StatModels. Now, it combines AR and MA parameters.

Now, you understand two of the three parameters of the ARIMA function, The p of the AR model and the q of the MA model.

Figure 8.10: Backtest ARMA model on the EURUSD

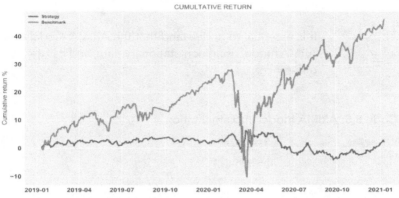

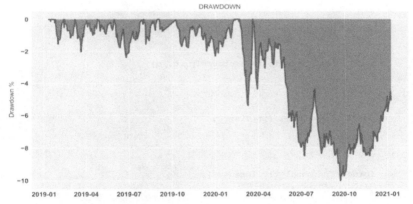

ARMA has been a combination of two losing models on this data. We have a bad return using the ARMA model in this example.

8.3.2. ARIMA model

We have seen enough ARMA models in this chapter. However, we need to understand the d parameter of the ARIMA model. If you remember the previous section skillfully, we have seen that the data need to be stationary to use the ARMA model.

However, in finance, most of the time, series is not stationary. So, we need to transform the data into a stationary time series. To do it, we use differencing. The differentiation is the price t-1 to price. The ARIMA function allows us to differ with parameter d. Usually, with financial time series, d=1 if we fit the ARIMA model using the price or d=0 if we use the asset's returns.

 It is essential to understand that the ARIMA model is an ARMA model using non-stationary data, and it is the only difference.

Code 8.5: ARIMA model implementation

```
def ARIMA_predict_value(train_set):
    """ Function for predict the value of tomorrow using AR model"""

    # Define model
    p = 1
    q = 1
    d = 1
    model = ARIMA(train_set, order=(p, d, q))

    # Fit the model
    model_fit = model.fit(disp=0)

    # Make forecast
    forecast = model_fit.forecast()

    return forecast[0][0]


def ARIMA_model(df,returns=True): 1
    """ Function to predict the test set with a ARIMA model """

    # Find the split
    split = int(len(df)*0.70)

    # Predict the price using AR function
    df['predicted_value'] = df['Adj Close'].rolling(split).\
apply(ARIMA_predict_value)
```

144

```
# Shift the predicted price by 1 period
df['predicted_value'] = df['predicted_value'].shift(1)


# Compute the returns of the asset
if returns:
    df['returns'] = df['Adj Close']
    df['signal'] = np.where(df.predicted_value > 0, 1, -1)
else:
    df['returns'] = df['Adj Close'].pct_change(1)
    df['signal']   =   np.where(df.predicted_value   >   df['Adj
Close'], 1, -1)


    df['strategy'] = df.signal.shift(1) * df.returns


    return df
```

1   Warning: we cannot call this function ARIMA because there will be
interference with this and the ARIMA function of StatModels.

Figure 8.11: Backtest ARIMA model on EURUSD

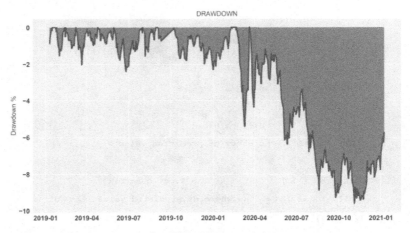

Same interpretation as for the ARMA model

Summary

- The log price properties are fascinating to understand the natural variation of the assets.

- The linear regression finds the line which minimizes the distance between all the observations.

- The Autoregressive model is a linear regression of the previous data. We can find the optimal lags using the partial autocorrelation graph.

- The moving average model uses the past error term to adjust the model. We can find the optimal lag using an autocorrelation graph.

- The ARMA model is a combination of the AR and the MA models. We can find the best parameters using the same criteria as for the AR and MA.

- The ARMA model needs stationary data. We can put the stock price in return to use it or use the ARIMA model, which allows us to add differentiation in the model to have stationary data.

Application Live Trading and Screener

This code is based on the class created in the annex: MetaTrader

Code 8.6: Application Trading / Screener for ARIMA model

```
from MT5 import *

import numpy as np

import pandas as pd

import warnings

warnings.filterwarnings("ignore")

from statsmodels.tsa.arima_model import ARIMA

import time


def sig_ARIMA_model(symbol):

    """ Function for predict the value of tommorow using ARIMA model"""


    train_set = MT5.get_data(symbol, 3500)["close"]
```

```python
    # Define model
    p = 1
    q = 1
    d = 1
    model = ARIMA(train_set, order=(p, d, q))

    # Fit the model
    model_fit = model.fit(disp=0)

    # Make forecast
    forecast = model_fit.forecast()

    value_forecasted = forecast[0][0]
    buy = train_set.iloc[-1] < value_forecasted
    sell = not buy

    return buy, sell

# True = Live Trading and False = Screener
live = True



if live:
    current_account_info = mt5.account_info()
    print("-----------------------------------------------------------")
    print("Date: ", datetime.now().strftime("%Y-%m-%d %H:%M:%S"))
    print(f"Balance: {current_account_info.balance} USD, \t"
          f"Equity: {current_account_info.equity} USD, \t"
          f"Profit: {current_account_info.profit} USD")
    print("-----------------------------------------------------------")


info_order = {
    "Euro vs USdollar": ["EURUSD", 0.01]
}
```

```python
start = datetime.now().strftime("%H:%M:%S")#"23:59:59"
while True:
    # Verfication for launch
    if datetime.now().weekday() not in (5,6):
        is_time = datetime.now().strftime("%H:%M:%S") == start
    else:
        is_time = False



    # Launch the algorithm
    if is_time:

        # Open the trades
        for asset in info_order.keys():

            # Initialize the inputs
            symbol = info_order[asset][0]
            lot = info_order[asset][1]

            # Create the signals
            buy, sell = sig_ARIMA_model(symbol)

             # Run the algorithm
            if live:
                MT5.run(symbol, buy, sell,lot)


            else:
                print(f"Symbol: {symbol}\t"
                    f"Buy: {buy}\t"
                    f"Sell: {sell}")
    time.sleep(1)
```

149

The live parameter sets the live trading mode (live = True) or the screener mode (live = False).

Chapter 9: Linear regression and logistic regression

This chapter discusses the regression model. First, we will go deeper into the simple linear regression. Then, we will see another class of predictive models, the classifiers.

9.1. Regression and classification

First, in this section, we will learn the difference between regression[12] and classification models.

9.1.1. Reminder about regression

In the previous chapter, we have done a little resume of the linear regression. Here, we will remind and explain how regression works for any regression algorithms.

- All regression models want to predict a continuous value. For example, if a model predicts the percentage of stock variation, the prediction will be contained into the interval [-30%; +30%], and it can take all values in this interval (for example, 1.57%, 6.78%, 13.39%).

- Intuitively, the idea of regression is to find a model which can be closer to each value of a dataset. We can compute the sum of the distance between the predicted value $\tilde{y}_i$ and the real value y_i using the mean squared error (MSE). Mathematically, MSE = $\sum(\tilde{y}_i - y_i)^2$

- All regression algorithms have their method to be optimized. However, all can be tested with the MSE to find if it is a good model or not. In comparison, the line regression is the only which optimizes the MSE to find the best parameters.

---

[12] **Additional lecture** : Linear Regression for Machine Learning, Jason Brownlee

9.1.2. Understand the classification

In this part, we will talk about the classification models. To understand it quickly, we will follow the same guideline as the previous reminder about linear regression to highlight the differences.

- When we work with a classification algorithm, the target is not a continuous value. Indeed, it is a definite value. For example, we can predict if the stock price will increase or decrease tomorrow but not predict a value. In classification, the target vector is 0 for the decreasing day and 1 for the increasing day.

- Naturally, the cross-entropy function is the most common to find the best parameters for this algorithm. It is a complicated name for a simple thing. This function calculates the percentage of the excellent prediction.

- The most used metrics to understand the performances of a classification model are the precision and confusion matrix.

Now, suppose we have understood all these points perfectly. In that case, we can ask ourselves: "Why was cross-entropy used to optimize the classification algorithm and not just the precision." We use the cross-entropy function to optimize because, in optimization, we need a continuous function like f(x) = x. Still, the precision is not continuous, so we need to find other solutions, and we find this solution using cross-entropy. The function is unimportant but is put for the one who wants to know it.

$$CE = -\sum_{c=1}^{M}\sum_{o=1}^{N} y_{o,c} \log(p_{o,c})$$

Where M is the number of classes, N is the number of observations, $y_{o,c}$ is the true observation and $\log(p_{o,c})$ is the predicted probability observation. We will go deeper into the predicted probability notion later in the chapter.

Now, let us talk about the testing-performances metrics for the classification. The best-known metric is precision. It is calculated by the number of true predictions divided by the number of predictions.

The confusion matrix has been explained as one of the best testing performance metrics. It is a matrix with true positive, false positive, false negative, and true negative. It is interesting to understand in which way the algorithm is wrong. Let us see in figure 9.1 a theoretical confusion matrix.

Figure 9.1: Theoretical confusion matrix

Real\Prediction	True	False
True	True positive	True negative
False	False negative	False positive

Moreover, the utilization of the confusion matric depends on the context. Suppose we work on an earthquake predictive algorithm. In that case, the worst value is the true negative because it means we do not predict the earthquake, but it happened. The False positives are wrong, but not really because we expected the earthquake, and it did not happen. Suppose the model predicts a corporate's upward trend the following year. In that case, True negatives are insignificant because we do not invest in this corporate, so we do not lose money instead of the False positive, which means we have invested in the wrong company.

9.2. Linear regression

In this section, we will learn how to perform a linear regression on the stock price. We will learn how to prepare the data, perform a linear regression, and backtest it.

9.2.1. Preparation of data

First, we need to import the data. We have chosen the EURUSD currency to be able to compare to the performance of the ARIMA model.

I work only with the percentage of variation because we do not need to standardize the data in many cases, and the variations are more representative than the stock price (we will explain this point in part 9.3.1).

In the data, we add a new column with yesterday's price. It will be the variable that we will use to predict the price of today. Let us see this in code 9.1.

Code 9.1: Import the data

```
# Import the data
df = yf.download("EURUSD=X", end="2021-03-01")[["Adj Close"]].\
pct_change(1)


# Create a X
df["Adj Close t-1"] = df[["Adj Close"]].shift(1) 1


# Drop missing values
df = df.dropna()
```

1   Add a shift to put the X (yesterday's return) and the y (today's return) of the same day on the same row.

In statistics and machine learning, the data are divided into X and y. X is all the variables that we use to predict the variable y. In our case, X is yesterday's return, and y is today's return. Moreover, we need to divide a train set and a test set. This decomposition allows us to train the model on the train set and test the performances on unknowing data, the test set. Usually, we use 80% of the data for the train set and 20% for the test.

Code 9.2: Creation of the train and test set

```
# Percentage train set
split = int(0.80*len(df))


# Train set creation
```

```
X_train = df[["Adj Close t-1"]].iloc[:split]
y_train = df[["Adj Close"]].iloc[:split]


# Test set creation
X_test = df[["Adj Close t-1"]].iloc[split:]
y_test = df[["Adj Close"]].iloc[split:]
```

You can use the train_test_split function of scikit-learn to do the same. Be sure that you understand the function because there are many subtilities in this function, as the possibility of doing a shuffle which is not good in finance (we do not want to predict the past with the future).

9.2.2. Implementation of the model

In this part, we implement the linear regression model. Before we begin the code, it is interesting to have the linear regression equation here because it is a straightforward equation (we do not do that with the other algorithms).

$$\tilde{y}_i = \beta_0 + \beta_1 x_{i,1} + \cdots + \beta_n x_{i,n}$$

Where the β_i are the parameters of the model, $x_{i,j}$ the observations from the dataset and $\tilde{y}_i$ the prediction. In our case the equation is:

$$r_{EURUSD,t} = \beta_0 + \beta_1 r_{EURUSD,t-1}$$

Where $r_{EURUSD,t}$ is the return of the EURUSD at time t.

Code 9.3: Linear regression implementation

```
# Import the class
from sklearn.linear_model import LinearRegression1


# Initialize the class
```

```
lr = LinearRegression() 2


# Fit the model
lr.fit(X_train, y_train) 3
```

1   Import the *LinearRegression* class from *scikit-learn.*

2   Instancy the class (Interesting when we have two models on different data).

3   Use the *fit()* command to train the coefficient of the linear regression.

 When the model is trained, we can use it to have the parameters (only for linear regression and some other algorithms) and make predictions.

Using the command *lr.coef_* and *lr.intercept_* we can find the parameters of the linear regression equation:

$$r_{EURUSD,t} = 3.53e^{-05} + -0.21_1 r_{EURUSD,t-1}$$

9.2.3. Predictions and backtest

This part will use the model implemented in the last part to make predictions and backtest the strategy.

We will use the predict command of the class lr to make predictions. Then, we need to find out how to code our strategy. It is easy. We buy if the predicted return is positive and sell if it is negative. We backtest using the function of chapter 5.

Code 9.4: Predictions and backtesting

```
# Create predictions for the whole dataset
df["prediction"] = lr.predict(df[["Adj Close t-1"]]) 1
```

```
# Compute the strategy
df["strategy"] = np.sign(df["prediction"]) * df["Adj Close"]2
```

```
# Backtest
backtest_dynamic_portfolio(df["strategy"].iloc[split:]) 3
```

1   Use the *predict()* command of the class *lr* to predict the future variations.

2   We do not need to put a *shift(1)* because it is put at the X.

3   Backtest only for the values after the split (test set).

Figure 9.2: Backtesting strategy created using linear regression on EURUSD

Beta: -0.0	Alpha: -2.33 %		Sharpe: -0.34	Sortino: -0.509
VaR: 17.93 %	cVaR: 20.23 %		VaR/cVaR: 1.128	drawdown: 21.15 %

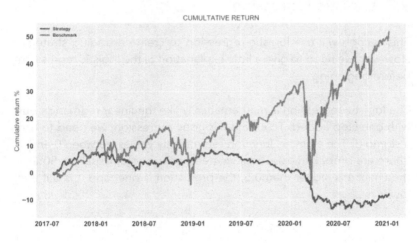

CUMULTATIVE RETURN

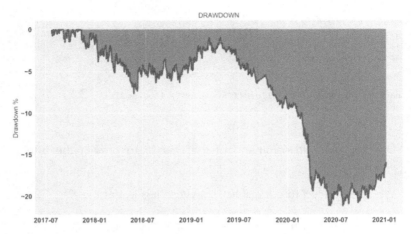

This figure shows that the performance is bad. Indeed, there is a negative Sharpe ratio, which means we lose money if we choose this strategy. Moreover, we lose money from the beginning: it is easy to see using the drawdown graphic.

9.3. Logistic regression

This section will use logistic regression to create a trading strategy. However, we need to give a little explanation of the logistic regression before beginning.

The logistic regression is mathematically like the linear regression but with one step added. To create a logistic regression, we need to use a sigmoid. The sigmoid function returns only values between 0 and 1 (there are probabilities). Then, we need a threshold. Usually is 50%. If the chance is higher than 0.5, the prediction is one, and it is 0 if it is lower.

$$\tilde{y}_{i, \, continious} = \beta_0 + \beta_1 x_{i,1} + \cdots + \beta_n x_{i,n}$$

$$\tilde{y}_{i, \, categorical} = \frac{1}{1 + e^{-\tilde{y}_{i, \, continious}}}$$

Where the β_i are the parameters of the model, $x_{i,j}$ the observations from the dataset, $\tilde{y}_{i, \, continious}$ the continuous prediction and $\tilde{y}_{i, \, categorical}$ the categorical prediction. Let us resume this in figure 9.3.

Figure 9.3: Logistic regression explanation

Linear regression   Sigmoid
prediction

9.3.1. Preparation of data

In this part, we will prepare the data for a classification algorithm. It is nearly the same as a regression algorithm. The difference is the target which needs to be a categorical variable.

There are many ways to process to create a categorical (or dummy) variable. The most useful is using the function where of numpy, which allows us to replace some value using conditions.

We will see in the next section how to use np.where. It is a little tricky as we work with stock returns. The stock has increased if the return was higher than 0 and decreased if the returns were lower than 0. So, suppose we add 0.5 to each value and round to the nearest integer. In that case, we have 1 for the increasing value and 0 for the decreasing value.

Code 9.5: data preparation for a classifier

```
# Percentage train set
split = int(0.75*len(df)) 1


# Train sets creation
X_train = df[["Adj Close t-1"]].iloc[:split]
y_train = np.round(df[["Adj Close"]].iloc[:split]+0.5)


# Test sets creation
X_test = df[["Adj Close t-1"]].iloc[split:]
y_test = np.round(df[["Adj Close"]].iloc[split:]+0.5)
```

1 We can choose 75% of the data for the train set. The rule to respect is that the train set must contain at least 70% and maximum 80% of the data.

9.3.2. Implementation of the model

The logistic regression class is from the library scikit-learn too. The syntax is the same as for the linear regression. So, we need to initialize the class and fit it using the X_train and y_train data.

Code 9.6: Logistic regression implementation

```
# Import the class
from sklearn.linear_model import LogisticRegression


# Initialize the class
lr = LogisticRegression()


# Train the model
lr.fit(X_train, y_train)
```

Model parameters exit:

```
LogisticRegression(C=1.0, class_weight=None, dual=False, fit_intercept=True,
                   intercept_scaling=1, l1_ratio=None, max_iter=100,
                   multi_class='auto', n_jobs=None, penalty='l2',
                   random_state=None, solver='lbfgs', tol=0.0001, verbose=0,
                   warm_start=False)
```

There are not many parameters for linear regression. So, it is better to analyze some parameters of this model. It is essential to understand that each model can be custom changing the parameters of the models. Suppose we create a logistic regression on the same data. In that case, the results can be different if we change the parameters. It is advised to consult the library's documentation to understand all the parameters. However, we are going to explain some essential parameters:

- **fit_intercept**: it can be true or false. We indeed have a β_0 in the linear regression equation. If it is false, we don't have one.

- **penalty:** if it is 'l2', the error function (the function we want to minimize) is an MSE. If it is 'l1', the error function is the MAE (mean absolute error).

- **verbose:** it can be 0 or 1. If it is 0, we cannot see details about the optimization of the algorithm. If it is 1, we have more information about the training.

It is interesting to change some parameters to improve your model, but if you adapt it too far from the data. The model can be unusable on other data. This problem is called overfitting, which is very active in finance because of the changing market situation.

9.3.3. Predictions and backtest

We analyze the strategy created using the logistic regression algorithm in this part. It will be the same as the linear regression, but after we will compare both algorithms.

Code 9.6: Logistic regression predictions

```
# Create predictions
df["prediction"] = lr.predict(df[["Adj Close t-1"]])


# Create the positions
df["prediction"] = np.where(df["prediction"]==0, -1, 1)


# Compute the returns of the strategy
df["strategy"] = np.sign(df["prediction"]) * df["Adj Close"]
```

We have used the function of numpy to give an example of power of this function.

Figure 9.4: Cumulative return of the strategy using logistic regression

Beta: 0.055	Alpha: 7.27 %		Sharpe: 0.596	Sortino: 1.06
VaR: 20.77 %	cVaR: 24.91 %		VaR/cVaR: 1.199	drawdown: 29.08 %

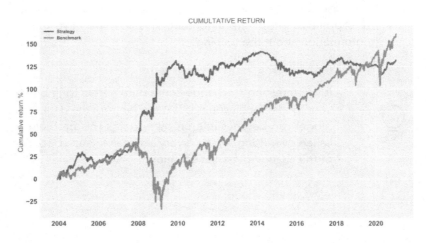

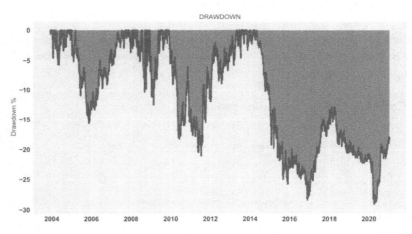

It is a good backtest. We have good metrics but a high drawdown (usually before a combination of strategies). The negative point is that the growth of the cumulative returns has stopped since 2010. The issues can be solved by fitting the model again because there are six years without another fitting (not very realistic).

Summary

- Linear regression is the most easy-to-understand algorithm of regression. It is trained using the MSE.

- The logistic regression is the classification algorithm derivate from the linear regression. To find the class, it uses the sigmoid function.

- If we want to adjust the algorithm to the train data too much, it will be unusable to the test data. This problem is called overfitting.

Application Live Trading and Screener

This code is based on the class created in the annex: MetaTrader

Code 9.7: Application Trading / Screener for logistic regression

```python
from MT5 import *
import numpy as np
import numpy as np
import pandas as pd
import warnings
warnings.filterwarnings("ignore")
from sklearn.linear_model import LogisticRegression
import time
import pickle
from joblib import dump, load
import os


path = "" # Ex:
C:/Desktop/Python_for_finance_and_algorithmic_trading/ChapterN/Models
```

```python
def create_model_weights(symbol):
    """ Weights for Linear regression on the percentage change"""
    # Import the data
    data = MT5.get_data(symbol, 3500)[["close"]].pct_change(1)


    # Create new variable
    data["close t-1"] = data[["close"]].shift(1)


    # Split the data
    data = data.dropna()
    split = int(0.80*len(data))


    # Train set creation
    X_train = data[["close t-1"]].iloc[:split]
    y_train = np.round(data[["close"]].iloc[:split]+0.5)


     # Create the model
    alg = LogisticRegression()


    # Fit the model
    alg.fit(X_train, y_train)


    # Save the model
    alg_var = pickle.dumps(alg)
    alg_pickel = pickle.loads(alg_var)


    dump(alg_pickel ,os.path.join(path,f"Models/{symbol}.joblib"))




def log_reg_sig(symbol):
    """ Function for predict the value of tommorow using ARIMA model"""


    # Create the weights if there is not in the folder
    try:
        alg = load(os.path.join(path,f"Models/{symbol}.joblib"))
```

```python
    except:
        create_model_weights(symbol)
        alg = load(os.path.join(path,f"Models/{symbol}.joblib"))


    # Take the lastest percentage of change
    data = MT5.get_data(symbol, 3500)[["close"]].pct_change(1)
    data["close t-1"] = data[["close"]].shift(1)


    X = data["close t-1"].iloc[-1].reshape(-1,1)



    # Find the signal
    prediction = alg.predict(X)
    prediction = np.where(prediction==0, -1, 1)
    buy = prediction[0][0] > 0
    sell = not buy



    return buy, sell

# True = Live Trading and False = Screener
live = True



if live:
    current_account_info = mt5.account_info()
    print("-----------------------------------------------------------")
    print("Date: ", datetime.now().strftime("%Y-%m-%d %H:%M:%S"))
    print(f"Balance: {current_account_info.balance} USD, \t"
            f"Equity: {current_account_info.equity} USD, \t"
            f"Profit: {current_account_info.profit} USD")
    print("-----------------------------------------------------------")



info_order = {
    "Euro vs USdollar": ["EURUSD", 0.01]
}
```

165

```python
start = datetime.now().strftime("%H:%M:%S")#"23:59:59"
while True:

    # Verfication for launch
    if datetime.now().weekday() not in (5,6):

        is_time = datetime.now().strftime("%H:%M:%S") == start
    else:

        is_time = False




    # Launch the algorithm
    if is_time:


        # Open the trades
        for asset in info_order.keys():
            # Initialize the inputs
            symbol = info_order[asset][0]
            lot = info_order[asset][1]


            # Create the signals
            buy, sell = log_reg_sig(symbol)


             # Run the algorithm
            if live:

                MT5.run(symbol, buy, sell,lot)


            else:

                print(f"Symbol: {symbol}\t"

                      f"Buy: {buy}\t"

                      f"Sell: {sell}")
    time.sleep(1)
```

The live parameter sets the live trading mode (live = True) or the screener mode (live = False).

Part 3: Machine learning, deep learning, live trading

This part will discuss implementing the most famous machine learning algorithms for trading: support vector machine, decision tree, random forest, etc. Then we will learn how to create some of the most powerful algorithms: deep neural network, recurrent neural network, and recurrent convolutional neural network. Moreover, we will implement a whole project using portfolio management, statistics, and machine learning algorithms.

Summary:

Chapter 10: Features and target engineering

Chapter 11: Support vector machine (SVM)

Chapter 12: Ensemble methods and decision tree

Chapter 13: Deep neural network (DNN)

Chapter 14: Recurrent neural network (RNN)

Chapter 15: Recurrent convolutional neural network (RCNN) *BONUS*

Chapter 16: Real life full project realization

Chapter 17: From nothing to live trading

Chapter 10: Features and target engineering

Classic data such as OHLCV are like a dismantled car, i.e., we cannot go anywhere. That is why we need to assemble the car (features engineering) to be able to drive. To find the destination, we will use the target engineering.

10.1 Motivation and intuition

Features and target engineering is one of the essential parts. Even if we have the most powerful algorithm if we give it to garbage input, we will have garbage output.

10.1.1 Features engineering

Let us give a simple example to understand better what features engineering is. Imagine that we want to predict the time we will take to go from point A to point B, and the only features we have at this step are the longitude and latitude of the two points. So, in our database, we have 5 columns: longitude_start, latitude_strat, longitude_end, latitude_end, and travel_time.

The question is: How can we help our algorithm better predict travel time with the longitude and attitude data? An example of that will be to compute the distance in kilometers between the start and the end point for each travel. We will find an excellent relation between the new feature (distance) and the target (travel time).

Features engineering can also allow us to find the best features for our problem by looking at the variance of the features. However, these methods are not relevant in trading because we will carefully create new variables to give more information to our algorithms about trends, short-term movement, volatility, etc.

Most of the new features in trading are technical indicators, price action figures, or quantitative metrics. Here are some metrics that will give some ideas for projects:

- **Quantitative features**: The variation from the N previous period to now, moving correlation between two columns. It will allow us to understand the short and long-term trend.

- **Price action patterns:** Detect some patterns to give us information about the downward and upward forces in the market, like engulfing and doji.

- **Technical indicators:** They are very versatile and can help us understand volatility, volume variation, and momentum.

To conclude, features engineering is the heart of our trading prediction problem because data is essential in data science. So, we have to choose features carefully!

The best way to create new features is by adding your own experience. Choose indicators that you know are important for the problem.

10.1.2 Target engineering

Features engineering is the car, but we will not go anywhere without a clear goal. That is why we need a clear target. So, we need to do some target engineering.

Understanding that the best features are nothing if we do not know the target is essential. Retaking our example of the car, if we want to go to a fantastic mountain spot, we should take a 4x4 vehicle instead of a racing car because the 4x4 vehicle is more adapted to the target (rough and winding terrain).

In trading, it is the same thing; we cannot create one set of features for all our algorithms because the goal of each of them is not the same. So, before creating the features, we need to choose the target. Let us give some examples of target engineering for a better understanding:

Triple barrier method: Highlight by Marco Lopez de Prado is a common technique to create a dummy variable containing -1 if we touch barrier 2, 0 if we touch barrier 3, and 1 if we touch barrier 1(Figure 10.1). If we work with a sell position, we need to inverse Barrier 1 and 2.

Figure 10.1: Triple barrier method with barrier 1 crossed

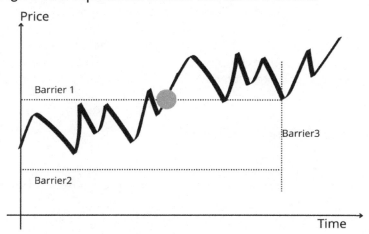

- **Variation threshold**: we look at the next N candles and compute the variation from now to in N candles to obtain a regressive target.

10.1.3 Why is it so important?

Even if we have said that many times before, the features and target engineering are essential. Here, we will create the "problem" to define which variable we want to predict (the target) using which features.

Once we have good features, finding a good predictive model is straightforward. However, if we do not have good data, we can create the more complex algorithm that we can, but it will not be capable of predicting something.

In our car example, the model is like the car tires; even if we keep our summer tires in winter, we can go anywhere we want. We will take more time and increase the accident risk. So, finding the model adapted to our problem is essential. However, it will be easy to find with good features and clear target.

Indeed, suppose we have a poor-quality data import. In that case, even if we have perfect features engineering, it will not be easy to have good results, and it is the same for the following step.

Moreover, as the features and target engineering are one of the first steps of a project, but not less important because we spend 80% of the time on a project on this step, it is essential to do it carefully.

10.2 Trading application

This section will apply the theory that we have spoken about previously. We will see how to create some interesting features and some relevant targets.

10.2.1 Create trading indicators and useful trading features

We will split this subsection into quantitative features, price action patterns, and technical indicators. The list that will be given is not exhaustive, so feel free to test many others to find the best.

Quantitative features
N previous days: it is one of the most accessible variables but also one of the most important because it will allow us to understand the previous long or short-term variation depending on the period we take.

Code 10.1: N previous day variation computation

```
# N previous days variation
n = 10
df[f"var_{n}"] = df["Adj Close"].pct_change(n)
```

Moving correlation: For this example, we will choose to compute the moving correlation between the 10 previous day variations and the

200 previous day variations. We do that to understand the relation between the long-term trend and the short-term behavior. It is an exciting feature for a machine learning algorithm (from my experience).

Code 10.2: Moving correlation computation

```
# Moving correlation
col_1 = "var_200"
col_2 = "var_10"
df["moving_correlation"] = df[col_1].rolling(50).corr(df[col_2])
```

Price action patterns

Doji: generally, we say that doji's express indecision. That is why we do not classify the doji as increasing doji or decreasing doji like in the following figure. It is helpful for the algorithm to understand when the investors are indecisive because it can show us the end or the start of a trading trend.

Code 10.3: Doji computation

```
# DOJI
df["DOJI"] = ta.CDLDOJI(df["Open"], df["High"], df["Low"], df["Close"])
```

 To detect the Doji, we use the Python TA-lib library because it is always better to use the library: you will minimize the error risk and optimize your code.

Figure 10.2 Some Doji examples

We can see that the sign of the candle does not mean anything to the Doji because it gives us indecision movement.

Engulfing pattern: There are two different engulfing patterns: the bullish and the bearish engulfing. We can see graphically both in Figure 10.3 and how to compute them without a library in Code 10.4.

Figure 10.3: Engulfing patterns

Bearish engulfing   Bullish engulfing

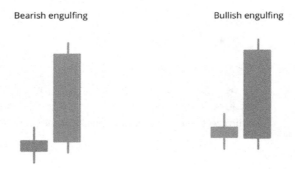

Graphically we speak about engulfing when the close price of the previous candle is nearly equal to the opening of the actual candle. Moreover, the actual candle must be greater than the previous.

Code 10.4: Engulfing computation

```
# ENGULFING
df["candle_way"] = -1
df.loc[(df["Open"] - df["Close"]) < 0, "candle_way"] = 1
```

```python
# Amplitude
df["amplitude_abs"] = np.abs(df["Close"] - df["Open"])
df["Engulfing"] = 0

df.loc[
        # Yersteday red candlestick and Today increase
        (df["candle_way"].shift(1) == -1) &\
        (df["candle_way"] == 1) &\


        # Close of the last decreasing candlestick = Open of today
    increase candlestick
        (df["Close"].shift(1) < df["Open"]*(1+0.5/100)) &\
        (df["Close"].shift(1) > df["Open"]*(1-0.5/100)) &\


        # Last decreaing candlestick is less strong than the Today
    increasing candlestick
        (df["amplitude_abs"].shift(1)*1.5  <  df["amplitude_abs"]),
    "Engulfing"] = 1

df.loc[
        # Yersteday green candlestick and Today decrease
        (df["candle_way"].shift(1) == 1) &\
        (df["candle_way"] == -1) &\


        # Close of the last decreasing candlestick = Open of today
    decrease candlestick
        (df["Close"].shift(1) < df["Open"]*(1+0.5/100)) &\
        (df["Close"].shift(1) > df["Open"]*(1-0.5/100)) &\


        # Last decreaing candlestick is less strong than the Today
    candlestick
        (df["amplitude_abs"].shift(1)*1.5  <  df["amplitude_abs"]),
    "Engulfing"] = -1
```

As we can see, this simple figure has several lines of code. That is why it is much better to use a library or create our function if we want to find a specific pattern.

Technical indicators

Resistance: The resistance can be computed using a lot of different ways. This book will use the max value over the last 150 periods. The support is the same thing but using the minimum.

Code 10.5: Resistance computation

```
# Max value in the last n days
n = 150
df["resistance"] = df["Close"].rolling(n).max()
```

Relative Strength Index (RSI): It will allow us to understand if the market is in an overbought or overselling market. So, it is ideal to have these features; for example, combining a doji can better predict the retracement.

Code 10.6: RSI computation

```
# RSI
n = 15
df["RSI"] = ta.RSI(df["Close"], timeperiod=n)
```

 To create technical indicators, you can use TA-lib. It will allow you to create nearly 100 indicators for your trading strategies.

10.2.2 Target labeling

As we said before, features are nothing if we do not create an interesting label. In this subsection, we will create classifier and regressor targets. All targets will be derived from the variation percentage, but obviously, we can create the target that we want; for example, we can predict a chart figure and try to detect if, after this figure, there is an increase or a decrease in the price.

First, we will compute the future N-day variation. We need to shift the data to align features and targets on the same row, but we will explain this more in detail in section 11.1.

Code 10.7: Futures N days variation

```
""" Next N days variations """
n = 1
df[f"target_var_{n}"] = df["Close"].pct_change(n).shift(n) 1
```

1   We put the *shift(n)* to not create interference in the data (like predict the past using the future)

Once we have this metric, creating a dummy variable to use a classifier algorithm will be easy. For example, we can create a dummy variable with only 2 values: -1 if the future return over N days is negative and 1 if it is positive.

Code 10.8: Futures N days variation (dummy variable)

```
""" Next N days variations (dummy)"""
n = 1
df[f"target_var_{n}"] = df["Close"].pct_change(n).shift(n)

df["target_dummy"] = 1
df.loc[df[f"target_var_{n}"]<0, "target_dummy"] = -1
```

However, with this technique, it cannot be easy to profit when the market is broad because the variation will be positive, but the variation will be minimal. So, to avoid having this issue, we can create a dummy variable with three values: -1, 0, and 1.

To do it, we will compute the percentiles 33 and 67. However, it is essential to compute the percentiles using the train set not to create any interference in the future (test set). Then, suppose the value is below percentile 33. In that case, we classify it as -1, if it is between percentile 33 and percentile 67 as 0, and 1 if it is greater than percentile 67.

Code 10.9: Futures N days variation (dummy variable bis)

```python
""" Classify the variations"""
    # find the variations
    n = 1
    df[f"target_var_{n}"] = df["Close"].pct_change(n).shift(n)



    # Find the centile 33 and 67 on the train set
    split = int(0.80*len(df))
    centile_33                                                    =
    np.percentile(df[[f"target_var_{n}"]].iloc[:split].dropna(), 33)
    centile_67                                                    =
    np.percentile(df[f"target_var_{n}"].iloc[:split].dropna().values,
    67)


    # Dummy variable
    df["target_dummy"] = 0
    df.loc[df[f"target_var_{n}"]>centile_67, "target_dummy"] = 1
    df.loc[df[f"target_var_{n}"]<centile_33, "target_dummy"] = -1
```

Summary

- OHLCV data are like dismantled car, so it is necessary to transform them.

- Features engineering helps the algorithm to better understand the relation between the data (is like assemble the car)

- Target labeling is the variable we want to predict (is where we want to go)

Chapter 11: Support vector machine (SVM)

This chapter discusses one of the most used algorithms in finance, the support vector machine. It is advantageous in finance because it does not need much data to train. Before learning SVM, we will make a point about data preprocessing. Then, we will learn how to use a support vector machine regressor (SVR) and a support vector machine classifier (SVC).

11.1. Preparation of data

In this section, we will prepare the data for our SVM[13] and recap what we already know about data preparation. Then we will go deeper into the concept explaining the data standardization.

11.1.1. Features engineering

In this section, we will quickly recap the data preparation. Indeed, we will do the same as in the previous chapters. So, we need to define sets of training and sets of tests. Furthermore, we will improve the features of our model. To do it, we will add some technical indicators. We do not explain the technical indicators that we will not use into the book. If you want to find some documentation about this, we can find it on internet and in books. We make a features engineering reminder here to truly understand how to incorporate it into our project.

---

[13] **Additional lecture** : Support-vector machine, Wikipedia

Features engineering helps the algorithm to find the best pattern in the data. For example, the stock price if you have an asset with a price between 50$ and 5000$, the model's parameters cannot be fit correctly. Instead of this, use the percentage variation which turns all assets into the same range. It is very helpful for the algorithm.

To create technical indicators, there are two ways. First, we can create by ourselves.

We can also use the technical analysis library of Python (ta). In this part, we will create the needed indicators by ourselves.

For this example, we have created a mean of returns and volatility of returns. These indicators cannot be found in the ta library, so we need to compute them ourselves. Moreover, we have put two timeframes on each indicator.

Code 11.1: Features engineering

```
# Features engeeniring
df["returns t-1"] = df[["returns"]].shift(1) 1


# Mean of returns
df["mean returns 15"] = df[["returns"]].rolling(15).mean().shift(1)
df["mean returns 60"] = df[["returns"]].rolling(60).mean().shift(1)


# Volatility of returns
df["volatility returns 15"] = df[["returns"]].rolling(15).std()
.shift(1)
df["volatility returns 60"] = df[["returns"]].rolling(60).std()
.shift(1)
```

1   It is expected as this step because we have seen it many times, but the shift to the feature columns allows us to put the X and the y on the same day in the same row.

Do not forget to add a shift to these indicators to not interfere in the data. Let us see why in figure 11.1

Figure 11.1: How to avoid interferences in the data

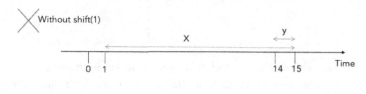

This figure shows that if we do not shift the data, we will have interferences because we predict the 15th day while we already have the 15th day in the features. It cannot be accurate, and we can lose much money if we make this error.

11.1.2. Standardization

This subsection will explain the concept of standardization. We see this in the SVM chapter because it is a geometric algorithm, and it is necessary to standardize the data for these algorithms. Still, we can apply this method to another algorithm.

The standardization allows doing the computation faster. Thus, it is interesting for the algorithm which demands many resources.

Sometimes like with this dataset, the data are not at the same scale. For example, we can have a volatility of 60% with a return of 1.75%. So, the algorithm has many difficulties working with that. We need to standardize the data to put it on the same scale. Let us see graphicly why we need to standardize the data in figure 11.2.

Figure 11.2: How standardization works?

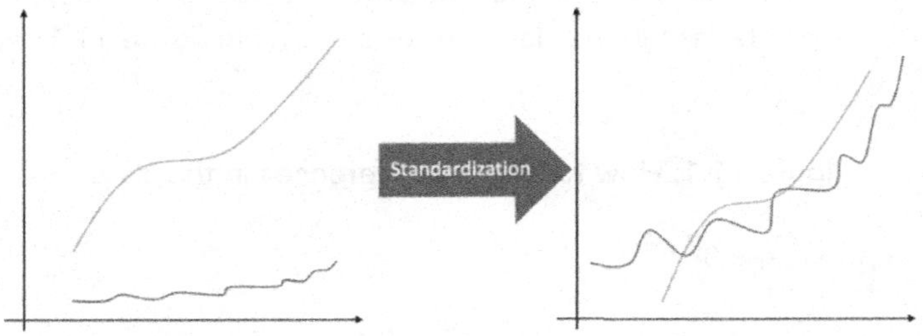

Standardization

This figure shows that it is difficult for us to understand the pattern between the two lines before standardization. It is also for the algorithm. Thus, we need to standardize the data to help us to understand it better.

Now, let us see the formula to standardize the data and standardize the data using Python.

$$z_i = \frac{x_i - \mu_x}{\sigma_x}$$

Where z_i is the standardize value, x_i is the value of the observation, μ_x is the mean of the vector x and σ_x the volatility of the vector x.

Code 11.2: Standardize the data

```
# Import the class
from sklearn.preprocessing import StandardScaler


# Initialize the class
sc = StandardScaler()


# Standardize the data
X_train_scaled = sc.fit_transform(X_train)
X_test_scaled = sc.transform(X_test)
```

 As for the other algorithms, we need to fit on the train set only because we cannot know the test set's mean and standard deviation in real life.

I never standardize the y because it does not intervene in the calculations. It is only used to calculate the model's error except for some specific models.

11.2. Support Vector Machine Classifier (SVC)

This section will explain how an SVC works, then how to create an SVC using Python and make predictions with the SVC to create a trading strategy.

11.2.1. Intuition about how works an SVC

In this part, we will see the intuition behind the support vector machine classifier.
To do it, we are beginning with a little graphic to understand what the SVC wants to do.

Figure 11.3: Functioning of an SVC

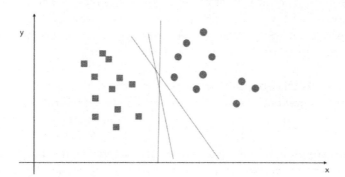

In this figure, we can see the question to which the SVC replies: "**How can the groups of points be separated optimally?**".

183

We use margins to find the optimal line between the two groups. These margins want to maximize the distance between the two groups. Then, we will take the middle of the two margins to find the delimitation for the two groups. Moreover, we will see that the points on the margins are called supports, and these points are the only important points in the algorithm. If we remove all the other points, the performance of the algorithm will be the same.

Figure 11.4: Optimize the distance

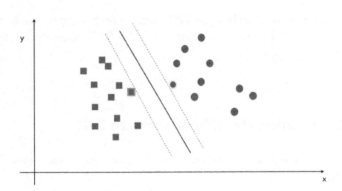

In this figure, we can see the functioning of an SVC and the supports.

The issue is that if a squared is in the circle group, the algorithm cannot run. It is because the algorithm has hard margins. Fortunately, it is possible to create an SVC with soft margins to avoid this problem.
With scikit-learn, it is possible to manage the margin encroachment. Suppose we put a C with a high value; we will not allow the model to have much margin encroachment. However, the more the value is low, the more the margin encroachment is significant.

Now let us talk about the kernel of the model. The kernel is the way that our algorithm is training. There are many ways to optimize an SVC, but the most used is the Gaussian kernel or the linear kernel in finance.

There are other kernels available on scikit-learn like a sigmoid kernel. However, we will see only the linear and the gaussian. A line like in figure 11.4 schematizes the linear, but the gaussian can keep a non-linear pattern like in figure 11.5.

Figure 11.5: Gaussian kernel schematization

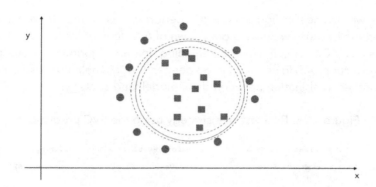

In this figure, we can see the functioning of an SVC using a Gaussian kernel.

11.2.2. How to create an SVC using Python

We will compute a Support Vector Machine Classifier (SVC) in this part using Python. It is effortless because it follows the same syntax as the logistic regression. We need to change the function to use the SVC function of scikit-learn.

Code 11.2: SVC implementation

```python
# Import the class
from sklearn.svm import SVC


# Initialize the class
svc = SVC()


# Fit the model
svc.fit(X_train_scaled, y_train_cla)
```

 We will use an SVC with an RBF kernel, the Gaussian kernel on scikit-learn.

185

11.2.3. Predictions and backtest

As we can see in figure 11.6, the performances of the strategy are terrible because we have a drawdown of 67% (confer the code) and a loss of 60%. So, if we are searching for an algorithm to put in production, we do not need to go deeper. It would help if we explored another combination between data, model, and strategy.

Figure 11.6: Backtest of a strategy using the SVC predictions

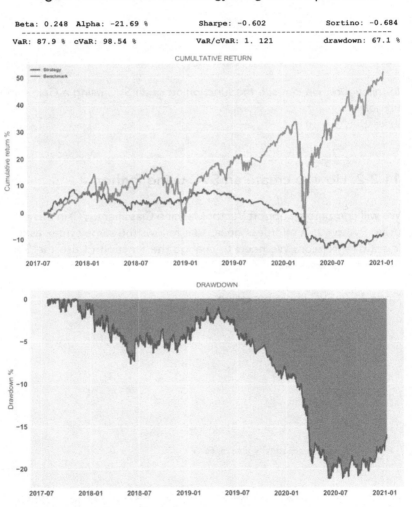

The constant growth of the drawdown is the worst thing that can happen to a strategy. Thus, it is a very bad strategy.

11.3. Support Vector Machine Regressor (SVR)

In this section, we will explain the intuition of the Support Vector Machine Regressor (SVR), then create the model and make a trading strategy using the prediction of our SVR.

11.3.1. Intuition about how works an SVR

It will be easy to understand because the SVR follows nearly the same process as the SVC. We need to take the problem in another way. Instead of maximizing the distance between two groups, the SVR tries to maximize the number of observations between the margins or minimize the number of observations outside the margins. Let us see an example in figure 11.7.

Figure 11.7: Intuition about SVR

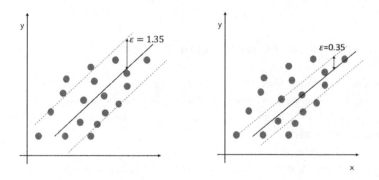

In this figure, we can see the functioning intuition of the SVR. The most useful parameter is the epsilon because it manages the path of the SVR.

The parameter epsilon is the tolerance of the model. It can be changed using the hyperparameter of the scikit-learn function. Many functions allow us to find the best combination between the hyperparameters of the models (we will see a technique in the next chapter) but do not forget that the more you optimize the algorithm to fit our data, the more the risk of overfitting increases.

11.3.2. How to create an SVR using Python

In this part, we want to create an SVR model using scikit-learn. To do it, we will use the SVR class of scikit-learn.

Code 11.3: SVR implementation

```
# Import the class
from sklearn.svm import SVR


# Initialize the class
svr = SVR()


# Fit the model
svr.fit(X_train_scaled, y_train_reg)
```

11.3.3. Predictions and backtest

We can mention that the features are the same for both. In comparison, the performance of the models is very different. Let us see figure 11.8. It is because of the target labeling (this time, the regressor is better).

As we can see, the regressor model wins 35% simultaneously as the classifier model loses 60% of the initial capital. However, why does nearly the same algorithm have some significant differences? The truth is that we cannot say why. Whereas, to avoid having some algorithms

188

with an awful performance like the SVC model, we can do a deep backtest to find the best algorithms that can be used to minimize the risk of losing money. We can also do a portfolio of strategies to reduce the risk and have more stable returns.

Figure 11.8: Cumulative return of the strategy using the SVR predictions

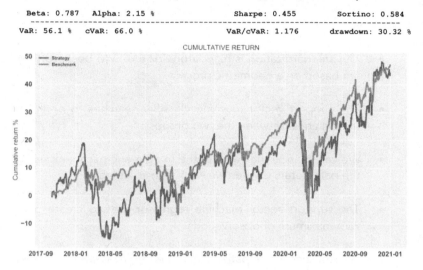

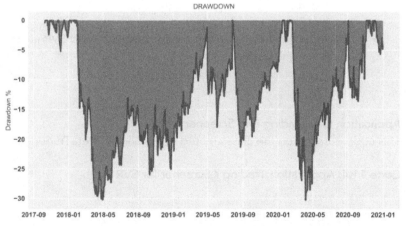

The strategy has a very good Sharpe ratio because it begins to be reasonably close to 0.5 (sharpe=0.45). It is not significantly correlated to the market (beta=0.787). However, many fluctuations in the cumulative returns imply a considerable risk of losses (cVaR = 66%). It is an excellent strategy to a portfolio of strategies to decrease the risk

because now this strategy is too risky, considering the overperform of the market.

Summary

- The standardization is mandatory for the SVM because they are based on a geometric process.

- The support vector machine classifier searches to optimize the distance between the two groups.

- We can change the value of the margin encroachment using the parameters C when we work with scikit-learn.

- The support vector machine regressor tries to create path with maximum of observations.

- We can change the path width using the parameter epsilon in scikit learn.

- The most used kernel in finance for both SVC and SVR is the linear and the gaussian kernel.

Application Live Trading and Screener
This code is based on the class created in the annex: MetaTrader

Code 11.4: Application Trading / Screener for SVR

```python
from MT5 import *

import numpy as np

import pandas as pd

import warnings

warnings.filterwarnings("ignore")

from sklearn.linear_model import LogisticRegression

import time

import pickle
```

```python
from joblib import dump, load
import os


path = "" # Ex: C:/Desktop/Python_for_finance_and_algorithmic_trading/
ChapterN/


def create_model_weights(symbol):
    """ Weights for Linear regression on the percentage change"""
    # Import the data
    data = MT5.get_data(symbol, 3500)[["close"]].pct_change(1)


    # Create new variable
    data["close t-1"] = data[["close"]].shift(1)


    # Split the data
    data = data.dropna()
    split = int(0.80*len(data))


    # Train set creation
    X_train = data[["close t-1"]].iloc[:split]
    y_train = np.round(data[["close"]].iloc[:split]+0.5)


     # Create the model
    alg = LogisticRegression()


    # Fit the model
    alg.fit(X_train, y_train)


    # Save the model
    alg_var = pickle.dumps(alg)
    alg_pickel = pickle.loads(alg_var)


    dump(alg_pickel ,os.path.join(path,f"Models/{symbol}.joblib"))




def log_reg_sig(symbol):
    """ Function for predict the value of tommorow using ARIMA model"""
```

191

```python
    # Create the weights if there is not in the folder
    try:
        alg = load(os.path.join(path,f"Models/{symbol}.joblib"))
    except:
        create_model_weights(symbol)
        alg = load(os.path.join(path,f"Models/{symbol}.joblib"))


    # Take the lastest percentage of change
    data = MT5.get_data(symbol, 3500)[["close"]].pct_change(1)
    data["close t-1"] = data[["close"]].shift(1)


    X = data["close t-1"].iloc[-1].reshape(-1,1)



    # Find the signal
    prediction = alg.predict(X)
    prediction = np.where(prediction==0, -1, 1)
    buy = prediction[0][0] > 0
    sell =not buy


    return buy, sell

# True = Live Trading and False = Screener
live = True



if live:
    current_account_info = mt5.account_info()
    print("-----------------------------------------------------------")
    print("Date: ", datetime.now().strftime("%Y-%m-%d %H:%M:%S"))
    print(f"Balance: {current_account_info.balance} USD, \t"
          f"Equity: {current_account_info.equity} USD, \t"
          f"Profit: {current_account_info.profit} USD")
    print("-----------------------------------------------------------")

info_order = {

    "Euro vs USdollar": ["EURUSD", 0.01]
```

```python
    }
start = datetime.now().strftime("%H:%M:%S")#"23:59:59"
while True:
    # Verfication for launch
    if datetime.now().weekday() not in (5,6):
        is_time = datetime.now().strftime("%H:%M:%S") == start
    else:
        is_time = False



    # Launch the algorithm
    if is_time:

        # Open the trades
        for asset in info_order.keys():

            # Initialize the inputs
            symbol = info_order[asset][0]
            lot = info_order[asset][1]

            # Create the signals
            buy, sell = log_reg_sig(symbol)

             # Run the algorithm
            if live:
                MT5.run(symbol, buy, sell,lot)


            else:
                print(f"Symbol: {symbol}\t"
                      f"Buy: {buy}\t"
                      f"Sell: {sell}")
    time.sleep(1)
```

The live parameter sets the live trading mode (live = True) or the screener mode (live = False).

Chapter 12: Ensemble methods and decision tree

In this chapter, we will see many algorithms of machine learning. First, we will see the decision tree, then the random forest, and some other ensemble methods instrumental in finance. All algorithms in this chapter will be applied to the Google stock price.

12.1. Decision tree

In this section, we will study the decision tree algorithm. This statistical machine learning algorithm is most useful in finance because it understands the nonlinear relationship between data.

12.1.1. Decision Tree classifier

We are beginning with the decision tree[14] classifier in this subsection. Before coding something, we will explain how a decision tree classifier works.

Mathematically, when we have a space with groups of points, the decision tree will cut the space with hyperplanes to separate the groups. A hyperplane is a line in a 2d space, so if we do not know what this means, remember it is a line in our example.

Moreover, each hyperplane is orthogonal to the others. What does it mean? In our case, each hyperplane is perpendicular to the others. It is essential to know that to understand the behavior of the algorithm. In the following figure, we will see how a decision tree works in an easier way.

---

[14] **Additional lecture** : Decision Trees in Machine Learning, Prashant Gupta

Figure 12.1: How works graphically a decision tree

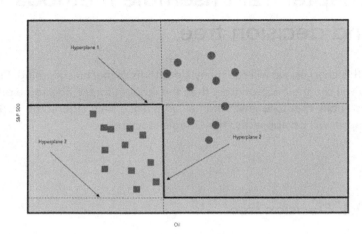

In this figure, we can see the different hyperplanes of the decision tree. In this example, there are three hyperplanes, meaning the depth of this decision tree is 3.

We will schematize the functioning of a decision tree to be sure we have understood what a decision tree classifier does. The decision tree works with conditions, let us see in figure 10.2.

Figure 12.2: Decision tree classifier

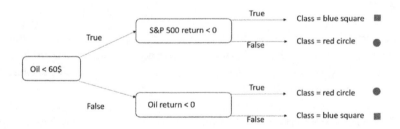

Besides that, it is a very interpretable model, which is interesting in finance. The decision trees do not need normalization to have good results. Moreover, it is a perfect algorithm when you have many dummy variables in features.

Now, we will see how to implement a decision tree classifier with Python. To do it, we import the DecisionTreeClassifier class of scikit-learn, and we will use the same syntax as for the previous algorithms.

Code 12.1: Decision tree classifier

```
# Import the class
from sklearn.tree import DecisionTreeClassifier


# Initialize the class
trc = DecisionTreeClassifier(max_depth=6)


# Fit the model
trc.fit(X_train, y_train_cla)
```

The hyperparameter max_depth is set at 6. However, it is a random choice. It is just not to let the tree go too deep because it is not good; we will see later why. We will see how to find the best depth in the next part.

Then, we have the model we can make predictions and backtest the strategy. As shown in figure 12.3, we have an excellent return using the depth of 6 because we have nearly 30% of returns yearly. Whereas, when we do not make precise the depth, the algorithm can go as deep as it wants, and it is not good; we can see that the returns of the same model but without precise the depth is -80% on the period.

Figure 12.3: Backtest depending on the depth max

Depth_max = 6

Beta: 1.056	Alpha: 12.44 %		Sharpe: 0.931	Sortino: 1.227
VaR: 41.76 %	cVaR: 52.03 %		VaR/cVaR: 1.246	drawdown: 30.79 %

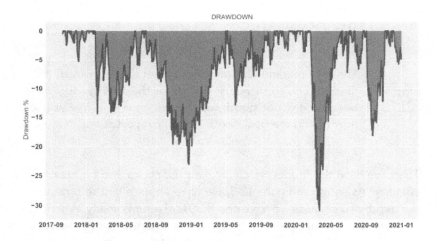

Depth_max = None

Beta: -0.034   Alpha: -20.95 %   Sharpe: -0.715. Sortino: -0.906

VaR: 91.56 %   cVaR: 101.59 %   VaR/cVaR: 1.11 drawdown: 57.31 %

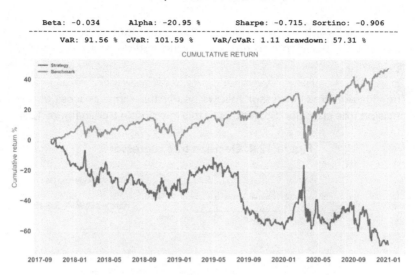

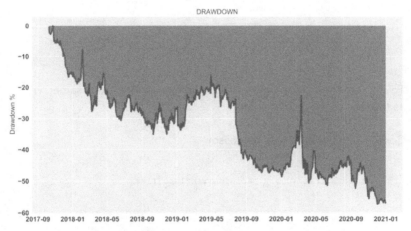

In this figure, we can see that the depth of the decision tree plays a crucial role. Indeed, the return difference between the two strategies is nearly 160% in the period. This highlights the overfitting problem when we let the algorithm with no depth restrictions.

The most critical hyperparameters in the decision tree are the depth of the tree which is given by the hyperparameter *max_depth* in scikit-learn.

12.1.2. Decision tree regressor

This part will explain how a decision tree regressor works and how to implement a decision tree regressor using Python and backtest the strategy.

The decision tree regressor follows nearly the same process as the decision tree classifier. So, let us see this in a simple tree in figure 12.4.

Figure 12.4: Decision tree regressor

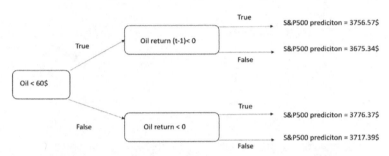

To implement a decision tree regressor, we will use the same syntax as the decision tree classifier.

Code 12.2: Decision tree regressor

```
# Import the class
from sklearn.tree import DecisionTreeClassifier


# Initialize the class
trc = DecisionTreeClassifier(max_depth=6)


# Fit the model
trc.fit(X_train, y_train_cla)
```

We can see the strategy results in figure 12.5, and as we can see with the constraint on the depth of the algorithm, it also gives good results.

Figure 12.5: Backtest strategy-based Google stock prediction

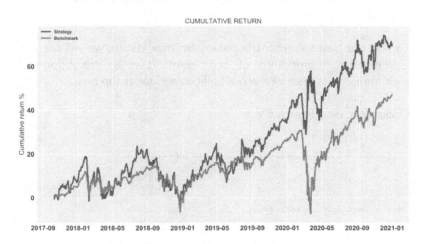

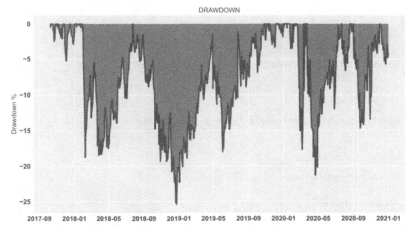

It is a very good backtest. We have a Sharpe ratio of 0.72 and an alpha at 18.27%, which means we overperform the market. However, we have a considerable drawdown. The best way to reduce the risk of a strategy is to combine it with the others, but we will see it later.

12.1.3. Optimize the hyperparameters

In the last part, we have said it is not an excellent choice to let the max depth without constraint, but we do not have to say how to find the optimal.

To find the best value for the parameter max_depth, we will use the GridShearchCV algorithm of scikit-learn. It is a straightforward algorithm. It just tests all the possibilities and takes the best.

Code 12.3: Grid Search CV

```
# Import the class
from sklearn.model_selection import GridSearchCV


# Create the model
dtr = DecisionTreeRegressor()


# Choose a list of parameters
param = {"max_depth": [3,6,15]} 1


# Create the GridSearch
model = GridSearchCV(dtr, param_grid=param, cv=3,)


# Train the model
model.fit(X_train.values, y_train_reg.values)


# Print best model
model.best_estimator_
```

Exit (best model):

```
DecisionTreeRegressor(ccp_alpha=0.0, criterion='mse', max_depth=3,
max_features=None, max_leaf_nodes=None,  min_impurity_decrease=0.0,
min_impurity_split=None, min_samples_leaf=1, min_samples_split=2,
min_weight_fraction_leaf=0.0, presort='deprecated',random_state=None,
splitter='best')
```

1   Create a dictionary containing all the variables we want to try with the different values. Here, we only want to test the test model depending on the maximum depth of the tree (3, 6, or 15).

As we can see, the best model is a length of 3. It is the best model on which criterion? As we do not have to specify, a criterion is the training criterion of the algorithm that will use the MSE. The wonderful thing is that we can customize the function to find the best algorithm using our criterion. We will create some criteria to explain this. The sum of the returns and the Sharpe ratio is proposed here, but we can create the ratio we want.

Code 12.4: Create new metrics

```
# Import the function
from sklearn.metrics import make_scorer


# RETURNS
# Create returns criterion
def returns(y, y_pred): 1

    return np.sum(np.sign(y_pred) * y)


# Transform criterion into a metric
returns_metric = make_scorer(returns, greater_is_better=True) 2


# SHARPE
# Create sharpe criterion
def sharpe(y, y_pred):

    r = np.sign(y_pred) * y

    return np.mean(r) / np.std(r) 3


# Transform criterion into a metric
sharpe_metric = make_scorer(sharpe, greater_is_better=True)
```

1 Criterion function for hyperparameters optimization takes only two input parameters: the real target and the predicted target.

2 The parameter greater_is_better highlights the algorithm if we want to maximize or minimize the metric.

3 It is unnecessary to annualize the Sharpe ratio here because the size relation does not matter. Thus, we add fewer things possible to optimize the time of computation.

> The function *make_score* allows us to transform a simple
> function into a metric compatible with the scikit-learn
> algorithms.

The function make_score allows us to transform a simple function into a metric compatible with the scikit-learn algorithms.

With the returns_metric and the sharpe_metric, we have an optimal depth of 3. It means that with the 3 ways, we have an optimal depth of three. So, we can say that in the training set, the best depth for the algorithm is 3.

12.2. Random Forest

This section discusses the random forest. First, we will see how to compute a random forest classifier, then a random forest regressor, and how to optimize the hyperparameters of a random forest.

12.2.1. Random Forest classifier

In this part, we will learn how to implement a random forest classifier. The random forest is the first ensemble method that we will learn. An ensemble method is a method that regroups algorithms to have a better prediction.

Naturally, as his name says, the random forest is an ensemble of decision trees. Indeed, the random forest is just an algorithm that combines the predictions of many decision trees to have better predictions.

We are not going deep in explaining the random forest because intuition is easy to understand. However, if we want to go deeper, we need much math, which is irrelevant to this book. Let us see the code of a random forest classifier.

Code 12.5: Random forest classifier

```
# Import the class
from sklearn.ensemble import RandomForestClassifier


# Initialize the class
lr = RandomForestClassifier()


# Fit the model
lr.fit(X_train, y_train_cla)
```

 Note that there is no hyperparameter custom here to show you the difference in figure10.6.

We will highlight the issue with the random forest (same as a decision tree) when you do not make precise the depth and the number of estimators (only for the random forest). There is big overfitting, as we can see in figure 12.6.

Figure 12.6: Highlight the overfitting

Train set backtest

Beta: -0.001	Alpha: 315.67 %	Sharpe: 14.104	Sortino: nan
VaR: -263.64 %	cVaR: -256.21 %	VaR/cVaR: 0.972	drawdown: -0%

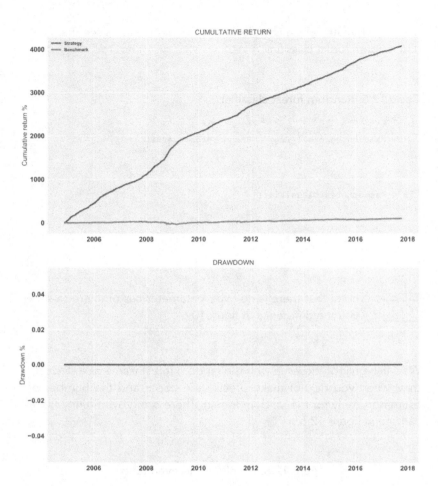

Test set backtest

```
      Beta: -0.018              Alpha: -6.45   Sharpe: -0.224  Sortino: -0.28
-------------------------------------------------------------------------------
VaR: 76.65 %          cVaR: 86.33 %        VaR/cVaR: 1.126      drawdown: 61.75 %
```

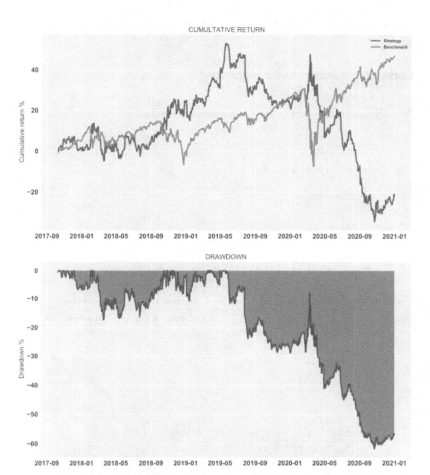

As we can see on the screen, there is overfitting because, in the train set (the data that the algorithm already knows), we win 350% per year with a drawdown of 0%, instead of the test set losing money.

12.2.2. Random Forest Regressor

In this part, we will about random forest regressors. Naturally, a random forest regressor is an ensemble of decision tree regressors.

We do not explain the same things to avoid being boring for this algorithm. We can copy exactly what we say for the random forest classifier on the random forest regressor. So, let us see how to implement it and highlight the overfitting problem of these algorithms again.

Code 12.6: Random forest regressor

```
# Import the class
from sklearn.ensemble import RandomForestRegressor


# Initialize the class
lr = RandomForestRegressor()


# Fit the model
lr.fit(X_train, y_train_reg)
```

Figure 12.7: Highlight overfitting on the random forest

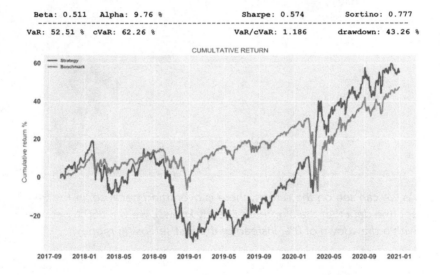

208

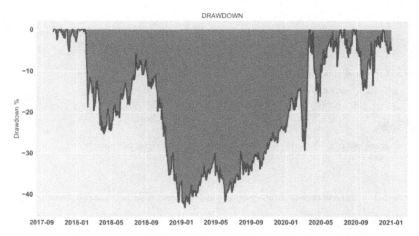

It is a good performance, but there is a significant drawdown over a very long period. It means that the strategy is perilous.

12.2.3. Optimize the hyperparameters

In this part, we will optimize the hyperparameters for the decision tree. For that, we will use the Sharpe metric used in part 12.1.3.

Code 12.7: Optimize the hyperparameters

```
# Import the class
from sklearn.model_selection import GridSearchCV


# Create the model
dtr = RandomForestRegressor()


# Choose a list of parameters
param = {"max_depth": [3,6,15], "n_estimators": [50, 100, 150]}



# Import the function
from sklearn.metrics import make_scorer
```

```
# SHARPE
# Create sharpe criterion
def sharpe(y, y_pred):
  r = np.sign(y_pred) * y
  return np.mean(r) / np.std(r)


# Transform criterion into a metric
sharpe_metric  = make_scorer(sharpe, greater_is_better=True)



model = GridSearchCV(dtr, param_grid=param, scoring=sharpe_metric,
cv=3)


model.fit(X_train.values, y_train_reg.values)


model.best_estimator_
```

 The parameters influencing a random forest are the number of trees and the deeper the trees are.

In the following figure, we can see that the tuning of the hyperparameters impacts the performances considerably. Indeed, this allows us to have a smoother curve and better backtest indicator.

Figure 12.8: Returns with and without tuning

Without tuning model

```
   Beta: -0.056    Alpha: 24.09 %    Sharpe: 0.776    Sortino: 1.143
-----------------------------------------------------------------------------
   VaR: 46.72 %    cVaR: 56.63 %    VaR/cVaR: 1.212    drawdown: 33.43 %
```

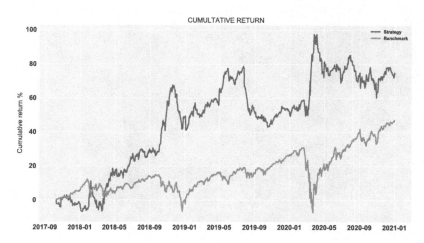

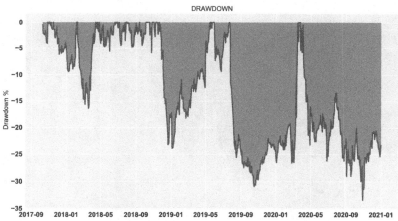

With tuning model

```
Beta: 0.553   Alpha: 18.25 %              Sharpe: 0.879      Sortino: 1.194
------------------------------------------------------------------------
VaR: 44.05 %  cVaR: 54.37 %               VaR/cVaR: 1.234    drawdown: 29.33 %
```

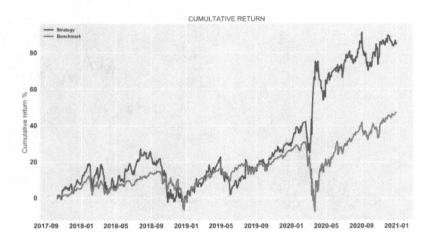

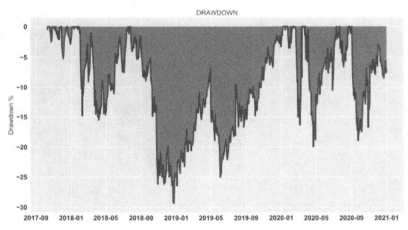

Unfortunately, for the example, the model without tuning is not overfitting because it has reasonable returns. However, the model with tunning is better because it has less drawdown, a higher Sharpe ratio, and fewer cVaR.

12.3. Ensemble methods

In this section, we will learn some ensemble methods[15]. First, we will see the simplest ensemble, the voting, the bagging, and the stacking methods.

12.3.1. Voting method

The voting method is the simplest method of the ensemble method. Let us see how it works in figure 12.9.

As we can see that the algorithms are well different, the prediction is better when we aggregate their prediction. However, we need some mathematical assumptions like the independence of the estimator. But, it is nearly impossible to have in real life because the algorithms train on the same data.

Figure 12.9: Voting classifier

					Count
True value	✗	✓	✗	✓	
SVC	✗	✗	✓	✓	2
Decision tree classifier	✗	✗	✗	✗	2
Random forest classifier	✓	✗	✗	✓	2
Voting classifier	✗	✗	✗	✓	3

As we can see in the figure the aggregation of the estimators is better than the estimators alone.

When we work with regression estimators, we follow the same process, except that the prediction is the mean of all predictions. Let

---

[15]**Additional lecture** : Ensemble Methods in Machine Learning: What are They and Why Use Them? Evan Lutins

us see a code for a VotingRegressor that uses LinearRegression, SVR, and RandomForestRegressor. Then we put the results in figure 10.10.

Code 12.8: Voting regressor implementation

```
from sklearn.linear_model import LogisticRegression

from sklearn.svm import SVR

from sklearn.ensemble import RandomForestClassifier,
VotingRegressor


# Intitialize the estimators
clf1 = LinearRegression()

clf2 = RandomForestRegressor(n_estimators=150, max_depth=3)

clf3 = SVR(epsilon=1.5)



# Create the ensemble method
eclf1 = VotingRegressor(estimators=[
        ('lr', clf1), ('rf', clf2), ("svc", clf3)]) 1


# Train the method
eclf1.fit(X_train, y_train_reg)
# Create predictions for the whole dataset
df["prediction"] = eclf1.predict(np.concatenate((X_train,X_test),
                                axis=0))


# Compute the strategy
df["strategy"] = np.sign(df["prediction"]) * df["returns"]


# Backtest
backtest_dynamic_portfolio(df["strategy"].iloc[split:])
```

1   Voting models are defined by a list of the estimators.

214

Figure 12.10: Cumulative returns of the voting regressor

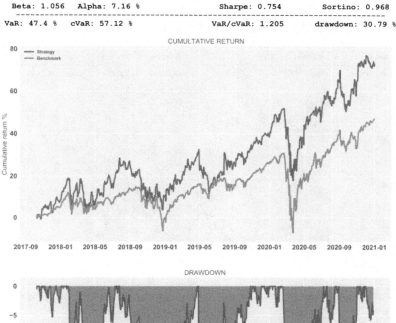

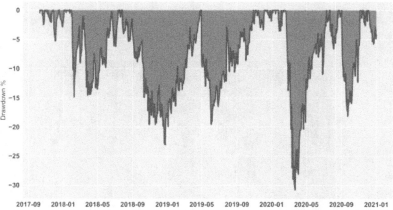

The voting method has similar results as the random forest, but the cumulative return is less volatile.

12.3.2. Bagging method

In this part, we will talk about the bagging method. It is a simple way to have an ensemble method in a few lines of code. Indeed, bagging

215

is a method that allows us to train an ensemble method with n same estimators. For example, a random forest is bagging with decision trees. Now, we will create a bagging regressor that uses 150 SVR.

Figure 12.11: Cumulative return of bagging using 150 SVR

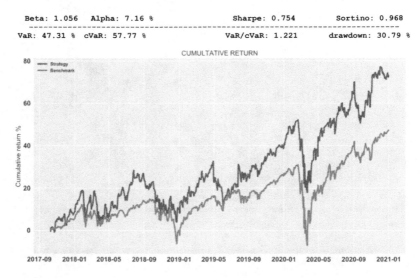

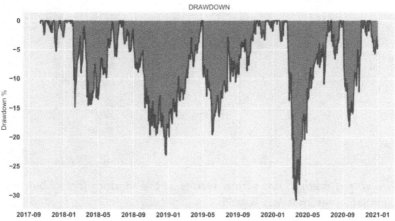

In this figure, we can see the cumulative return of a bagging algorithm created with 150 SVR.

Code 12.10: Bagging with SVR

```
from sklearn.svm import SVR

from sklearn.ensemble import BaggingRegressor


# Initialize the bagging
bag_reg = BaggingRegressor(SVR(epsilon=1.5), n_estimators=150)


# Train the method
bag_reg.fit(X_train, y_train_reg)


# Create predictions for the whole dataset
df["prediction"] = bag_reg.predict(np.concatenate((X_train,X_test),
                                    axis=0))


# Compute the strategy
df["strategy"] = np.sign(df["prediction"]) * df["returns"]

# Backtest
backtest_dynamic_portfolio(df["strategy"].iloc[split:])
```

12.3.3. Stacking method

In this part, we will talk about the stacking method. This method is a little different from the others because now, instead of doing a mean, for example, we will give the prediction of the estimators to another algorithm that will give the prediction.

Figure 12.12: Stacking method schematization

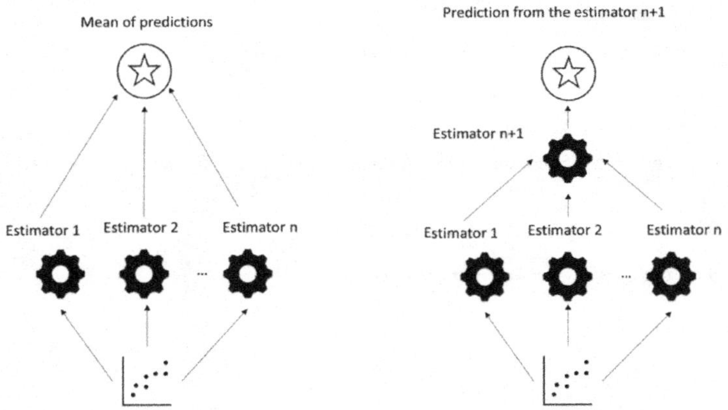

Mean of predictions

Prediction from the estimator n+1

Estimator n+1

Estimator 1   Estimator 2   Estimator n

Estimator 1   Estimator 2   Estimator n

This figure shows the difference between the voting and bagging (left), which do the mean of the estimator prediction instead of the stacking (right), which does an algorithm to aggregate the prediction better.

Usually, we put a decision tree or a random forest when we do a stacking classifier because they work very well with the dummy variable.

Code 12.11: Stacking regressor implementation

```
from sklearn.linear_model import LinearRegression

from sklearn.svm import SVR

from sklearn.ensemble import RandomForestRegressor,
StackingRegressor


# Intitialize the estimators
clf1 = LinearRegression()

clf2 = RandomForestRegressor(n_estimators=150, max_depth=3)

clf3 = SVR(epsilon=1.5)


# Create the ensemble method
eclf1 = StackingRegressor(estimators=[
        ('lr', clf1), ('rf', clf2), ("svc", clf3)])


# Train the method
```

```
eclf1.fit(X_train, y_train_reg)


# Create predictions for the whole dataset
df["prediction"] = eclf1.predict(np.concatenate((X_train,X_test),
                                        axis=0))


# Compute the strategy
df["strategy"] = np.sign(df["prediction"]) * df["returns"]


# Backtest
backtest_dynamic_portfolio(df["strategy"].iloc[split:])
```

Figure 12.11: Cumulative return of a stacking method

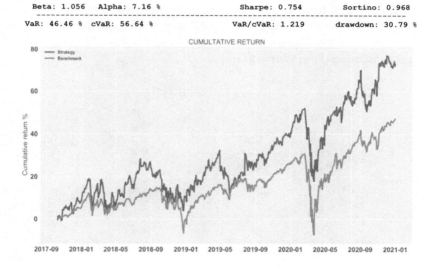

```
Beta: 1.056   Alpha: 7.16 %                    Sharpe: 0.754      Sortino: 0.968
------------------------------------------------------------------------------
VaR: 46.46 %  cVaR: 56.64 %                    VaR/cVaR: 1.219    drawdown: 30.79 %
```

219

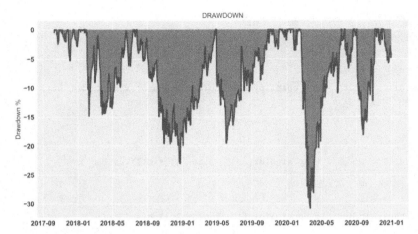

In this figure, we can see the cumulative return of a stacking regressor.

As we can see, the results of the ensemble methods are the same. It means that we cannot do a better prediction using this data with this type of algorithm. To avoid this issue, we will see something most powerful using deep learning later.

Summary

- To find the best separation between groups, the decision tree cut the space with n hyperplanes (where n is the depth of the tree).

- A random forest is an ensemble method (bagging) that uses a much different decision tree to have better predictions than a decision tree.

- The decision tree and random forest are very exposed to overfitting. To avoid that, we need to constrain the depth of the tree and the number of trees for the random forest.

- The voting methods combine some algorithms. It gives the mean of individual algorithm predictions for the regression and the most voted class for the classification.

- Bagging is an ensemble method that combines the exact algorithm n times (for example, random forest).

- Stacking is an ensemble method that uses an algorithm with the predictions of algorithms in features to find the best predictions.

Application Live Trading and Screener
This code is based on the class created in the annex: MetaTrader

Code 12.12: Application Trading / Screener for Decision Tree Regressor

```python
from MT5 import *

import numpy as np

import pandas as pd

import warnings

warnings.filterwarnings("ignore")

from sklearn.tree import DecisionTreeRegressor

import time

import pickle
```

221

```python
from joblib import dump, load

import os

from sklearn.preprocessing import StandardScaler


path = "" # Ex: C:/Desktop/Python_for_finance_and_algorithmic_trading/
ChapterN/


def create_model_weights(symbol):
    """ Weights for Linear regression on the percentage change"""
    # Import the data
    data = MT5.get_data(symbol, 3500)[["close"]].pct_change(1)


    # Create new variable
    data.columns = ["returns"]


    # Features engeeniring
    data["returns t-1"] = data[["returns"]].shift(1)


    # Mean of returns
    data["mean returns 15"] = data[["returns"]].rolling(15).mean()
.shift(1)
    data["mean returns 60"] = data[["returns"]].rolling(60).mean()
.shift(1)


    # Volatility of returns
    data["volatility returns 15"] = data[["returns"]].rolling(15).std()
.shift(1)
    data["volatility returns 60"] = data[["returns"]].rolling(60).std()
.shift(1)


    # Split the data
    data = data.dropna()
    split = int(0.80*len(data))


    # Train set creation
    X_train = data[["returns t-1", "mean returns 15", "mean returns 60",
            "volatility returns 15",
            "volatility returns 60"]].iloc[:split]
```

```python
        y_train = data[["returns"]].iloc[:split]


        sc = StandardScaler()

        X_train = sc.fit_transform(X_train)


        # Create the model

        alg = DecisionTreeRegressor(max_depth=6)


        # Fit the model

        alg.fit(X_train, y_train)


        # Save the model

        alg_var = pickle.dumps(alg)

        alg_pickel = pickle.loads(alg_var)


        dump(alg_pickel ,os.path.join(path,f"Models/{symbol}_reg.joblib"))


def tree_reg_sig(symbol):

    """ Function for predict the value of tommorow using ARIMA model"""


    # Create the weights if there is not in the folder

    try:

        alg = load(os.path.join(path,f"Models/{symbol}_reg.joblib"))

    except:

        create_model_weights(symbol)

        alg = load(os.path.join(path,f"Models/{symbol}_reg.joblib"))


    # Take the lastest percentage of change

    data = MT5.get_data(symbol, 3500)[["close"]].pct_change(1)


    # Create new variable

    data.columns = ["returns"]


    # Features engeeniring

    data["returns t-1"] = data[["returns"]].shift(1)


    # Mean of returns

    data["mean returns 15"] = data[["returns"]].rolling(15).mean()
```

223

```
.shift(1)

    data["mean returns 60"] = data[["returns"]].rolling(60).mean(
).shift(1)


    # Volatility of returns
    data["volatility returns 15"] = data[["returns"]].rolling(15).std()
.shift(1)
    data["volatility returns 60"] = data[["returns"]].rolling(60).std()
.shift(1)


    X = data[["returns t-1", "mean returns 15", "mean returns 60",
            "volatility returns 15",
            "volatility returns 60"]].iloc[-1:,:].values


    # Find the signal
    prediction = alg.predict(X)
    buy = prediction[0] > 0
    sell =not buy



    return buy, sell



# True = Live Trading and False = Screener
live = True


if live:
    current_account_info = mt5.account_info()
    print("-----------------------------------------------------------")
    print("Date: ", datetime.now().strftime("%Y-%m-%d %H:%M:%S"))
    print(f"Balance: {current_account_info.balance} USD, \t"
        f"Equity: {current_account_info.equity} USD, \t"
        f"Profit: {current_account_info.profit} USD")
    print("-----------------------------------------------------------")



info_order = {
    "Google": ["Alphabet_Inc_C_(GOOG.O).a", 1.00]
```

```
    }
start = datetime.now().strftime("%H:%M:%S")#"23:59:59"
while True:
    # Verfication for launch
    if datetime.now().weekday() not in (5,6):
        is_time = datetime.now().strftime("%H:%M:%S") == start
    else:
        is_time = False
    # Launch the algorithm
    if is_time:

        # Open the trades
        for asset in info_order.keys():

            # Initialize the inputs
            symbol = info_order[asset][0]
            lot = info_order[asset][1]

            # Create the signals
            buy, sell = tree_reg_sig(symbol)

             # Run the algorithm
            if live:
                MT5.run(symbol, buy, sell,lot)

            else:
                print(f"Symbol: {symbol}\t"
                    f"Buy: {buy}\t"
                    f"Sell: {sell}")
        time.sleep(1)
```

225

The live parameter sets the live trading (live = True) or the screener mode (live = False).

Chapter 13: Deep Neural Networks (DNN)

In this chapter, we see our first algorithm for deep learning. We will talk about the deep neural network DNN, or artificial neural network ANN. Deep learning is a field of machine learning which uses the most powerful algorithms. However, it demands many resources to run. To explain the DNN and create a trading strategy using this algorithm, we will explain the intuition behind the DNN and how to create a DNN classifier and a DNN regressor. Moreover, after this chapter, we will be capable of making our loss function. We will implement the algorithms on the Apple stock price.

13.1. Intuition behind DNN

This part will discuss the intuition behind the Deep Neural Network or DNN. To do it, we will speak about the forward propagation of a neural network, then about the gradient descent, and finally about the backpropagation.

13.1.1. Forward propagation

In this subsection, we will learn a lot about forwarding propagation which is the process used by the algorithm to create a prediction. The essential thing in this process is the neuron. Indeed, it is an essential part of understanding the concept of forwarding propagation. To begin, we explain how one neuron works.

One neuron is like linear regression. It has an input named X and a set of parameters to predict an output y. The parameters are named weights in deep learning, and the intercept (β_0 in the linear regression) is called bias. The only difference between the neuron and a linear regression is that we put in an activation function (we will discuss the action functions later). Let us see the process behind a neuron in figure 13.1.

Figure 13.1: Neuron process

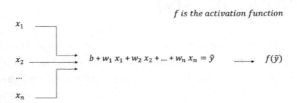

In this figure, we can see the process behind one neuron in a deep neural network.

Now, let us discuss the activation function. Usually, it is just a way to contain the value of the output. However, we will explain later that in the hidden layer, the choice of the activation function is not "really" essential but is crucial for the output layer. Let us see the different activation functions in figure 13.2 to understand the notion better.

Figure 13.2: Some activation function

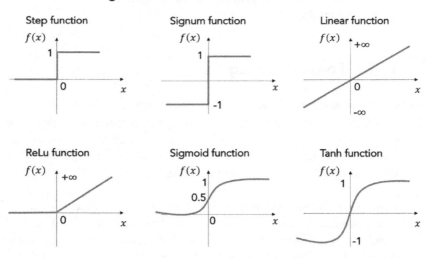

This figure shows some activation functions, whereas the most used are the ReLu, the linear, and the sigmoid function.

Now, we already know nearly all about the intuition behind forwarding propagation. The only thing that we need to know is how to combine neurons to create a neural network.

The construction of a neural network is straightforward. In figure 13.1, we have created one neuron with inputs and output. We must connect some neurons to create a neural network, like in figure 13.3. So, the output of the first neuron becomes the input of the following and so on until the output neuron.

Figure 13.3: Deep neural network

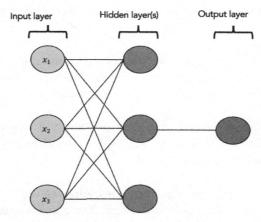

In this figure, we can see the functioning of a DNN. We see the input layer with the data, the hidden layer, and the output layer.

 As you can see, the interpretability of the model is tricky because there is a lot of computation and weight. So, some people in finance do not like the DNNs because it wants to know which criteria they will invest. However, the majority does not care.

So, forwarding propagation is to have data put into the neural network and give an output, the prediction. However, this process does not train our algorithm. So, in the following parts, we will see how to train the DNN.

13.1.2. Gradient descent

In this part, we will learn what gradient descent is. Gradient descent is the most popular algorithm in machine learning to optimize the weight of an algorithm. It is a way to solve an optimization problem.

The gradient descent is an algorithm based on the function's gradient that wants to optimize. This algorithm is mathematically easy-to-understand, but we need to use some very complex math to create it. So, we will see only the intuition here. However, if we want to go deeper into the subject, we can find much documentation about it on the internet.

We need to take a simple example to understand how gradient descent works. We are on a mountain and there is a vast mist. We want to get down the mountain but cannot see anything.

To do it, we will search only with our feet the way with the most downward slope, and we go in this direction after some meters; we will continue this process until we are down.

It is precisely what the algorithm does. After we want to check which way has the most downward slope, the algorithm uses the most negative gradient as we use our feet to find the most downward slope. The choice of the learning rate is essential. Let us see in figure 13.4 the importance of the learning rate.

Figure 13.4: Learning rate choice

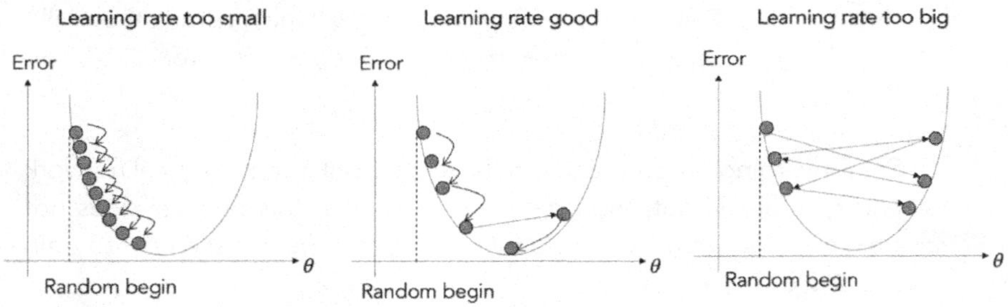

In this figure, we can see the importance of learning in the training process.

In deep learning, the letter θ represents all the weight of all neurons of the network. It is the parameters of the models. So, if we change θ, we change some or all weight and bias of the neurons.

The only problem with the gradient descent is that it can fall at a local minimum. To schematize the local and global minimum, we can think of a gold digger in a cave. There is a pack of 1kg gold (the local minimum) and only one pack of 100kg (the global minimum). Suppose we do not know that there is a pack in the cave. There is much chance of finding a pack of 1kg and leaving the cave without the pack of 100kg; this problem depends on the cost function. Usually, for a regression task, we use the MSE, which is convex, so there is no issue. However, the algorithm can fall at a local minimum if we create our loss function as in the next part.

Figure 13.5: Global minimum VS local minimum

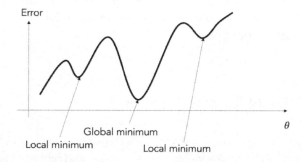

This figure shows that if the function is not strictly convex, the algorithm can fall into a local minimum even if there is a global minimum elsewhere.

To solve this problem, we can use stochastic gradient descent[16] or one other of these derivatives.

---

[16] **Additional lecture:** Stochastic Gradient Descent — Clearly Explained !!, Aishwarya V Srinivasan

13.1.3. Backpropagation

We will talk about backpropagation. At this step, we know all we must do to explain the backpropagation. We need to assemble the parts.

Figure 13.6: DNN training

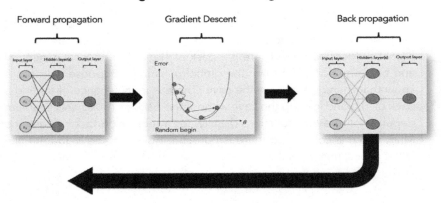

After seeing this figure, we can understand the definition of backpropagation: changing the weight after each iteration according to the gradient descent to optimize the algorithm and make better predictions in the future.

13.2. DNN for classification

This section will explain how to do a DNN correctly for a classification task using Python. We will prepare the data and highlight some points to know. Then we will implement the DNN and create a strategy with the prediction.

13.3.1. Preparation of data

In this subsection, we will discuss about the preparation of the data. As for the previous algorithms, the data will be split into train and test sets. We work at the Apple stock price with a daily timeframe.

Code 13.1: Preparation of the data

```python
# Import the data
df = yf.download("AAPL", end="2021-01-01")[["Adj
Close"]].pct_change(1)
df.columns = ["returns"]


# Features engeeniring
df["returns t-1"] = df[["returns"]].shift(1)


# Mean of returns
df["mean returns 15"] = df[["returns"]].rolling(15).mean().shift(1)
df["mean returns 60"] = df[["returns"]].rolling(60).mean().shift(1)


# Volatility of returns
df["volatility returns 15"] =
df[["returns"]].rolling(15).std().shift(1)
df["volatility returns 60"] =
df[["returns"]].rolling(60).std().shift(1)


# Drop missing values
df = df.dropna()


# Percentage train set
split = int(0.80*len(df))


# Train set creation
X_train = df[["returns t-1", "mean returns 15", "mean returns 60",
              "volatility returns 15",
              "volatility returns 60"]].iloc[:split]


y_train_reg = df[["returns"]].iloc[:split]


y_train_cla = np.round(df[["returns"]].iloc[:split]+0.5)


# Test set creation
```

233

```
X_test = df[["returns t-1", "mean returns 15", "mean returns 60",
             "volatility returns 15",
             "volatility returns 60"]].iloc[split:]


y_test_reg = df[["returns"]].iloc[split:]
y_test_cla = np.round(df[["returns"]].iloc[split:]+0.5)



# NORMALIZATION
# Import the class
from sklearn.preprocessing import StandardScaler


# Initialize the class
sc = StandardScaler()


# Standardize the data
X_train_scaled = sc.fit_transform(X_train)
X_test_scaled = sc.transform(X_test)
```

We do not explain this part because it is coded from the previous chapters. At the same time, it is essential to standardize our data when we work with a neural network because it is a very complex algorithm.

13.2.2. Implementing a DNN for a classification task

In this part, we will implement a DNN for a classification task. We will use TensorFlow to create the model. The deep learning algorithms demand a little comprehension to create them. So, ensure we understand the previous chapters before beginning.

Creating a model with TensorFlow gives us many possibilities. However, on the contrary, we need to understand what we want to do instead of the scikit-learn algorithm in which we have to put the data. However, do not worry, we are going to explain step by step the construction the different steps of the DNN.

Code 13.2: Deep neural network for classification task

```
# LIBAIRIES
import tensorflow
from tensorflow.keras.models import Sequential
from tensorflow.keras.layers import Dense


nb_hidden_layer = 1
```
1

```
# INTIALIZATION SEQUENTIAL MODEL
classifier = Sequential()
```
2

```
# ADD HIDDEN LAYER
for _ in range(nb_hidden_layer):
```
3
```
    classifier.add(Dense(75, input_shape = (X_train.shape[1],),
activation="relu"))
```
4

```
# OUTPUT LAYER DENSE
classifier.add(Dense(1, activation="sigmoid"))
```
5

```
# COMPILE THE MODEL
classifier.compile(loss="binary_crossentropy", optimizer="adam")
```
6

```
# TRAINING
classifier.fit(X_train_scaled, y_train_cla, epochs=15,
batch_size=32, verbose=1)
```
7

1   Define the number of hidden layers.

2   Initialize the neural network.

3   Create a loop that add the hidden layers.

4   *input_shape = (X_train.shape[1],)* is only necessary for the first layer.

5   It is necessary to put a sigmoid to the activation because it is a classifier.

235

6   Compilation of the model using the stochastic gradient and binary cross-entropy as loss function.

7   Fit the model using only verbose=1 to highlight the training of the model.

Now, we will explain this code. First, we need to initialize the model as for the scikit-learn models. After that, we have just an empty model; we need to build it. The loop allows us to create as hidden layers as we want. The Dense function of TensorFlow creates a layer of neural networks. We have to be precise about how many neurons we want, the shape of the inputs, and the activation function.

Then we need to define a particular layer for the output because we need to predict the class. So, we want to predict a 0 or a 1. We choose the sigmoid to activate this neuron because the value will be between 0 and 1, and we want a probability.

Then we have to explain how we want to train the algorithm. We choose the cross-entropy function and a stochastic descent gradient named "adam." To fit the model, we must choose the number of epochs and the batch_size.

We can put callbacks in the fit function to stop the algorithm to a certain level of function loss, but this is not relevant for this book. You can read the TensorFlow documentation for more details.

13.2.3. Prediction and Backtest

In this part, we will analyze the performance of a strategy created using a DNN. We are going to use precisely the same code as the previous backtest.

Code 13.3: Compute return strategy using the DNN predictions

```
# Create predictions for the whole dataset
df["prediction"] =
classifier.predict(np.concatenate((X_train,X_test),
```

```
                                        axis=0))
df["prediction"] = np.where(df["prediction"] == 0, -1,1)
# Compute the strategy
df["strategy"] = np.sign(df["prediction"]) * df["returns"]


# Backtest
backtest_dynamic_portfolio(df["strategy"].iloc[split:])
```

With this code, we can see backtest of a strategy using the DNN classifier on Apple stock. As we can see, there is an excellent performance because we win more than 30% annually. In comparison, we need to consider that we have not integrated the fees.

Figure 13.7: Backtest of a DNN prediction strategy on Apple stock

```
Beta: 1.23     Alpha: 17.49 %              Sharpe: 0.594        Sortino: 0.841
---------------------------------------------------------------------------
VaR: 84.73 %  cVaR: 100.5 %                VaR/cVaR: 1.186      drawdown: 81.8 %
```

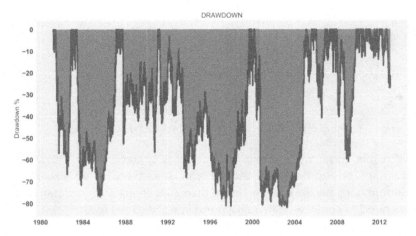

We can see a good trend in the growth of capital using this strategy.

13.3. DNN for regression

In this section, we will learn how to create a DNN for a regression task and how to create our loss function. Then, backtest the strategy.

13.3.1. Implementing a DNN for a regression task

In this part, we will create a DNN for a regression task. It is very similar to the classifier, but there are some subtilities. We only need to change the loss function to optimize the activation of the output neuron. Let us see the code then we will explain it more in detail.

Code 13.4: DNN regressor implementation

```
nb_hidden_layer = 1


# INTIALIZATION SEQUENTIAL MODEL
regressor = Sequential()


# ADD HIDDEN LAYER
for _ in range(nb_hidden_layer):
```

```
    regressor.add(Dense(75, input_shape = (X_train.shape[1],),
activation="relu"))

# OUTPUT LAYER DENSE
regressor.add(Dense(1, activation="linear"))

# COMPILE THE MODEL
regressor.compile(loss="mse", optimizer="adam")

# TRAINING
regressor.fit(X_train_scaled, y_train_reg, epochs=15,
batch_size=32, verbose=1)
```

 Here the activation function of the output neuron is essential. For example, if we put a sigmoid, the algorithm predicts only a positive return, which is impossible.

We have chosen to train the model using the Mean Squared Error (MSE) as a loss function.

 If we begin deep learning, it is advised to keep the linear activation function for the output of a regressor. If we understand the concept well, we can try a tanh function or others as seen before.

13.3.2. Custom loss function

We have seen how to train the model with a usual metric in the last part. At the same time, we can create our metrics if we want. The question is, why do we want to do that? Let's explain some limitations:
- We take the same investment if the algorithm predicts 15% or - 0.000001%.

- The error is almost the same for the MSE between 0.000001 or -0.000001.

We must therefore incorporate in our loss function that if the prediction is wrong in sign, we add a malus. We need to calculate the following equation in Tensorflow.

$$MSE_\alpha = \begin{cases} (y - \tilde{y})^2 \ if \ y * \tilde{y} > 0 \\ \alpha(y - \tilde{y})^2 \ if \ y * < 0 \end{cases}$$

Where $\tilde{y}$ is the prediction, y is the true value and $\alpha > 1$.

Code 13.5: Custom MSE function

```
def ALPHA_MSE(y_true, y_pred): 1

  y_true_roll = tf.roll(y_true, shift=1, axis=0) 2

  y_pred_roll = tf.roll(y_pred, shift=1, axis=0)

  y_true_dif = tf.math.sign(y_true_roll-y_true) 3

  y_pred_dif = tf.math.sign(y_pred_roll-y_pred)

  booleen_vector = y_true_dif == y_pred_dif 4

  alpha = tf.where(booleen_vector, 1, 3) 5

  alpha = tf.cast(alpha, dtype=tf.float32) 6

  mse = F.square(y_true-y_pred)

  mse = tf.cast(mse, dtype=tf.float32)

  scale_mse = tf.multiply(alpha, mse)

  alpha_mse = F.mean(scale_mse)

  return alpha_mse
```

1   Custom loss function needs to have two parameters *y_true* and *y_pred*, which are tensors. Thus, all the computations need to use TensorFlow functions.

2   Create a new variable containing the target shift by 1.

3   Take the sign of the daily variation.

4   *Create a Boolean tensor in which each value is True if y_true and y_pred varies in the same way and False neither.*

5   Create multiplicator vector, which is equal to 1 if the two vectors vary in the same way and 3 neither to penalize the wrong size.

240

6   Transform a tensor in a constant vector.

 This part is not mandatory for the book, but you should know that creating a custom loss function is possible. You can consult the TensorFlow documentation if you want to go deeper into the subject.

Keep in mind that customizing a loss function and creating a metric with scikit learn are two distinct things; do not confuse them. With the custom metrics of scikit-learn, we train a model using an MSE or another essential function and we take the best models following the created metrics. However, the loss function custom in TensorFlow is the function that computes the model's error (like MSE in scikit-learn).

13.3.3. Prediction and Backtest

In this part, we will backtest the strategy created using the custom loss and the strategy using the DNN training with MSE loss.

As we can see in the figure and as we have said in the last part, the custom loss is not for beginners. Indeed, the custom loss strategy is good but not better than the strategy using the MSE.

Figure 13.8: Backtest of the strategy using MSE and MSE alpha

MSE alpha

Beta: 1.127	Alpha: 15.55 %		Sharpe: 1.065	Sortino: 1.396
VaR: 36.33 %	cVaR: 45.6 %		VaR/cVaR: 1.255	drawdown: 38.52 %

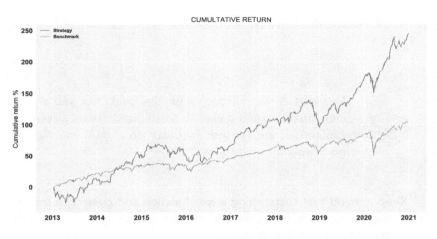

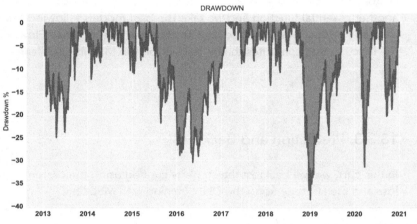

MSE

Beta: 1.127	Alpha: 15.55 %		Sharpe: 1.065	Sortino: 1.396
VaR: 36.33 %	cVaR: 45.6 %		VaR/cVaR: 1.255	drawdown: 38.52 %

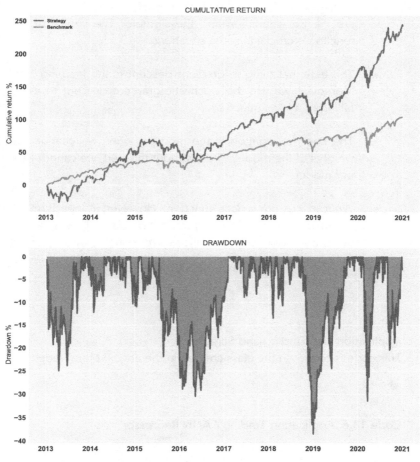

This figure shows that the custom loss function does not impact the performances because the two backtest are similar.

With the DNN, we have excellent results, but the DNN does not consider that we work with a time series.

Summary

- The process behind a neuron is like linear regression; instead of putting the y in a activation function.

- There are many activation functions. However, the most used are the ReLu function and the sigmoid. The choice of the function is crucial in some situations.

- The essential thing in gradient descent is the learning rate. Moreover, we use the stochastic gradient descent to avoid falling to a local minimum.

- The backpropagation is the moment when we change the weights of the model. Thus, without this part, we cannot train our model.

- We can custom a loss function. However, it needs much knowledge in deep learning to do it properly. Thus, if we are not comfortable with the notions of the books, we should not go into this subject.

Application Live Trading and Screener

This code is based on the class created in the annex: MetaTrader

Code 13.6: Application Trading / ANN Regressor

```python
from MT5 import *

import numpy as np

import pandas as pd

import warnings

warnings.filterwarnings("ignore")

import time

import pickle

from joblib import dump, load


import os

from sklearn.preprocessing import StandardScaler

import tensorflow

from tensorflow.keras.models import Sequential

from tensorflow.keras.layers import Dense
```

```
path = "" # Ex: C:/Desktop/Python_for_finance_and_algorithmic_trading/
ChapterN/



def ANN():
    # Create the model
    nb_hidden_layer = 1



    # INTIALIZATION SEQUENTIAL MODEL
    alg = Sequential()



    # ADD HIDDEN LAYER
    for _ in range(nb_hidden_layer):
        alg.add(Dense(75, input_shape = (5,), activation="relu"))



    # OUTPUT LAYER DENSE
    alg.add(Dense(1, activation="linear"))


    # COMPILE THE MODEL
    alg.compile(loss="mse", optimizer="adam")
    return alg


def create_model_weights(symbol):
    """ Weights for Linear regression on the percentage change"""
    # Import the data
    data = MT5.get_data(symbol, 3500)[["close"]].pct_change(1)


    # Create new variable
    data.columns = ["returns"]


    # Features engeeniring
    data["returns t-1"] = data[["returns"]].shift(1)


    # Mean of returns
```

245

```python
    data["mean returns 15"] = data[["returns"]].rolling(15).mean()
.shift(1)
    data["mean returns 60"] = data[["returns"]].rolling(60).mean()
.shift(1)


    # Volatility of returns
    data["volatility returns 15"] = data[["returns"]].rolling(15).std()
.shift(1)
    data["volatility returns 60"] = data[["returns"]].rolling(60).std()
.shift(1)


    # Split the data
    data = data.dropna()
    split = int(0.80*len(data))


    # Train set creation
    X_train = data[["returns t-1", "mean returns 15", "mean returns 60",
             "volatility returns 15",
             "volatility returns 60"]].iloc[:split]
    y_train = data[["returns"]].iloc[:split]


    # Initialize the class
    sc = StandardScaler()


    # Standardize the data
    X_train = sc.fit_transform(X_train)


    alg = ANN()


    # TRAINING
    alg.fit(X_train, y_train, epochs=13, batch_size=32, verbose=1)


    # Save the model
    alg.save_weights(os.path.join(path,f"Models/ANN_reg_{symbol}"))

def ANN_cla_sig(symbol):
    """ Function for predict the value of tommorow using ARIMA model"""
```

```python
# Create the weights if there is not in the folder
try:
    alg = ANN()
    alg.load_weights(os.path.join(path,f"Models/ANN_reg_{symbol}"))
except:
    create_model_weights(symbol)
    alg = ANN()
    alg.load_weights(os.path.join(path,f"Models/ANN_reg_{symbol}"))


# Take the lastest percentage of change
data = MT5.get_data(symbol, 3500)[["close"]].pct_change(1)
# Create new variable
data.columns = ["returns"]


# Features engeeniring
data["returns t-1"] = data[["returns"]].shift(1)


# Mean of returns
data["mean returns 15"] = data[["returns"]].rolling(15).mean()
.shift(1)
data["mean returns 60"] = data[["returns"]].rolling(60).mean()
.shift(1)


# Volatility of returns
data["volatility returns 15"] = data[["returns"]].rolling(15).std()
.shift(1)
data["volatility returns 60"] = data[["returns"]].rolling(60).std()
.shift(1)


X = data[["returns t-1", "mean returns 15", "mean returns 60",
          "volatility returns 15",
          "volatility returns 60"]].iloc[-1:,:].values


# Find the signal
prediction = alg.predict(X)
prediction = np.where(prediction==0, -1, 1)
buy = prediction[0][0] > 0
sell = not buy
```

247

```
        return buy, sell



# True = Live Trading and False = Screener
live = True


if live:
    current_account_info = mt5.account_info()
    print("-----------------------------------------------------------")
    print("Date: ", datetime.now().strftime("%Y-%m-%d %H:%M:%S"))
    print(f"Balance: {current_account_info.balance} USD, \t"
          f"Equity: {current_account_info.equity} USD, \t"
          f"Profit: {current_account_info.profit} USD")
    print("-----------------------------------------------------------")



info_order = {
    "Apple": ["AAPL.a", 1.00]
}



start = datetime.now().strftime("%H:%M:%S")#"23:59:59"
while True:
    # Verfication for launch
    if datetime.now().weekday() not in (5,1):
        is_time = datetime.now().strftime("%H:%M:%S") == start
    else:
        is_time = False



    # Launch the algorithm
    if is_time:



        # Open the trades
        for asset in info_order.keys():
```

```python
# Initialize the inputs
symbol = info_order[asset][0]
lot = info_order[asset][1]



# Create the signals
buy, sell = ANN_cla_sig(symbol)

 # Run the algorithm
if live:
    MT5.run(symbol, buy, sell,lot)

else:
    print(f"Symbol: {symbol}\t"
        f"Buy: {buy}\t"
        f"Sell: {sell}")
time.sleep(1)
```

 The live parameter sets the live trading (live = True) or the screener mode (live = False).

Chapter 14: Recurrent neural network

In this chapter, we will talk about Recurrent Neural Networks (RNN). This algorithm specialized in time series can be a precious ally in creating a trading strategy because the asset prices are time series. Moreover, it is one of the most complex deep learning algorithms. We will implement the strategies using the Netflix stock.

14.1 Principles of RNN

In this section, we will learn how an RNN works. Here, we will see the basis of RNN, but you may check some internet papers if you want to go deeper into the subject.

14.1.1. How an RNN works

This part will discuss the intuition behind the RNN. RNN models are specialized in time series modeling. Indeed, the network structure is slightly different from the ANN because the hidden layers are interconnected.

The interconnection between the hidden layer allows the model to "remember" the past. In the RNN, there are two types of memory instead of the ANN. The RNN has its long-term memory but also a short-term memory created by the interconnection that we speak previously.

We need a little representation to understand better how an RNN works. To do it, we need to simplify the representation of the ANN. We will schematize the ANN only with his layer and not all neurons. It allows us to visualize the model straightforwardly to create the representation for the RNN easier. Let us see figure 14.1.

Figure 14.1: New schematization of the ANN

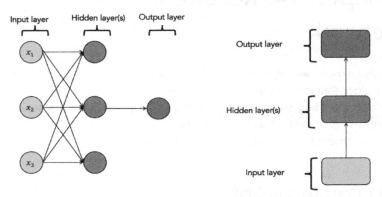

This figure showed the representation of an ANN using the layer only with the square instead of the left with all neurons. However, it is the same ANN.

Figure 14.2: Schematization of RNN

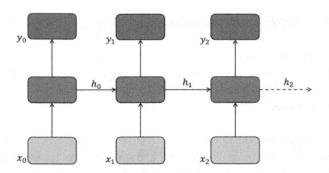

As we can see, the RNN is nothing else that ANN connected. We see that the information of the hidden layer is given directly to the next hidden layer, and it is not integrated only with the weights of the models.

The problem with the RNN is that the model may have some problems with the gradient since there are many more derivations than in the ANN case, which can cause vanishing gradient issues. At the same time, the researchers have found a solution to this problem. They have created new neurons named Long Short-Term Memory (LSTM) neurons. It is slightly different from the structure of a neuron we see in the last secion, so we need to study it.

14.1.2. LSTM neuron

How does an LSTM cell work? Naturally, it is not a deep learning course. So, if you want to understand the LSTM cell better, you need to go on the internet because this subject is irrelevant to this book. Let us know what it looks like for an LSTM cell. Then, we explain the difference between the dense and LSTM cells.

Figure 14.3: LSTM cell

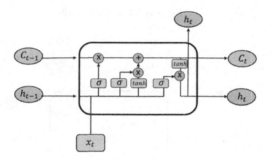

This figure shows the functioning of an LSTM cell where the memory at time t is C_t, and the information at time t is h_t. So, we can say that there are a long-term and short-term memory.

To better understand the LSTM cell, we will take a little example. Suppose we have an algorithm that predicts the next word, for example. We need C, which is the sentence, and h, which is some adjective, and x, the previous word.

The sigma is the sigmoid activation function. The most adds information it works like a plumbing valve it will let the information pass or not using the property of the sigmoid function.

So we don't go any further. It is understandable that this notion is not understood. However, this section only gives us some information to better understand how we are going to create the strategy using the

RNN and not be a complete deep learning course. If you don't understand this explanation, don't worry, we can continue the book without understanding it.

14.1.3. GRU cell

In this part, we will see derivatives of the LSTM neuron, the Gated Recurrent Unit (GRU). It is an excellent alternative to the LSTM because it takes only the information from the previous neuron and not the memory, which can be problematic in our case. Indeed, suppose we remember how the market reacted 15 years ago. In that case, it will not be the same as the market's reaction now because the market institutions have changed, the technologies have been evolved, etc.

Figure 14.4: GRU cell

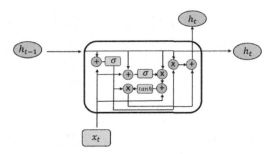

As we can see in the GRU cell, only the information h, we do not consider the memory C_t instead as in the LSTM.

 Even if the GRU and the LSTM differ, you must test both when creating your trading strategy on an RNN model.

In this section, we have seen much information about RNN. We can reread this section if we are uncomfortable with this notion or go to the next section because the theory is necessary to understand what we do but not to create the model. After all, we already know the functioning of an ANN. The RNN is similar even if it has some specificities. Now, we are ready to begin the code of the RNN using TensorFlow.

14.2. RNN for classification

We will see how to transform our data into 3d data (necessary for classification and regression and implement our model) and how to backtest the created strategy.

14.2.1. Transform 2d data to 3d data

This part will explain why and how to transform our 2d data into 3d data. If we have understood the theory behind the RNN very well (even if it is very hard with the information that is given you), we have understood that this network takes for each x, a matrix of shape (lags, m) where lag is the number of lag and m is the number of features. So, if we have n observations, we have a matrix with a shape (n, lags, m). Figure 14.5 represents the database we need.

Figure 14.5: Schematization of the data for an RNN

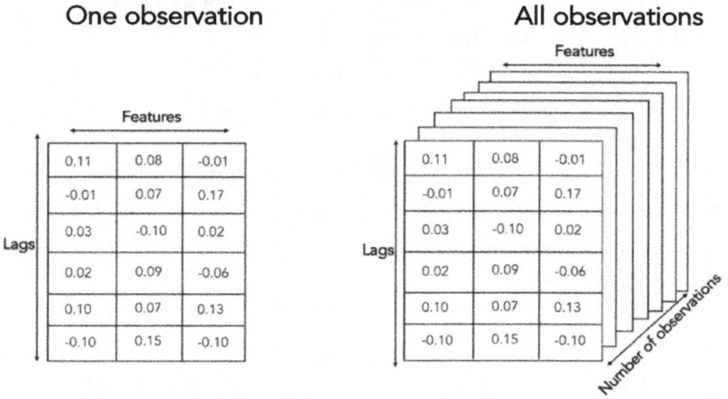

As we can see, the database for an RNN needs to be 3-dimensional. It is the same rules as for the ANN. However, for the ANN, we have a line as observation, so a 1-dimensional array, and when we have more than one, the matrix becomes 2-dimensional, instead of the RNN,

255

which needs a 2-dimensional array BY observation. Naturally, if we have more than one, the array will be 3-dimensional.

Code 14.1: Transform 2d data into 3d data

```
def X_3d_RNN(X_s, y_s, lag):

  # Simple verification
  if len(X_s) != len(y_s):
    print("Warnings")

  # Create the X_train
  X_train = []
  for variable in range(0, X_s.shape[1]):
      X = []
      for i in range(lag, X_s.shape[0]):
          X.append(X_s[i-lag:i, variable])
      X_train.append(X)
  X_train, np.array(X_train)
  X_train = np.swapaxes(np.swapaxes(X_train, 0, 1), 1, 2)

  # Create the y_train
  y_train = []
  for i in range(lag, y_s.shape[0]):
      y_train.append(y_s[i, :].reshape(-1,1).transpose())
  y_train = np.concatenate(y_train, axis=0)
  return X_train, y_train
```

 To check if X_train and y_train have the same size, we display a message but we don't raise an error because for some reason we can use X_train and y_train with different lengths.

We note that the y_train shape will not change, but we put it into the function to shift the value due to the lag. Now, we have the data in a suitable format. We can begin to implement the RNN classifier using TensorFlow.

14.2.2. Implementing the model

Creating the network in Python will be very similar to the ANN. So, we will only highlight the new points. With the LSTM function, we have a new argument which is *return_sequences*. To make it easy, if this parameter is false, we will return a 2-dimensional array, and if it is True, we will return a 3-dimensional array. So, we need to put it in the right place. If we do not use our loss function, we will have no issue with that, but if we use our loss function, we need to use this parameter correctly.

Code 14.2: RNN classifier

```
# LIBAIRIES
import tensorflow
from tensorflow.keras.models import Sequential
from tensorflow.keras.layers import Dense, LSTM


# INITIALIZATION OF THE MODEL
classifier = Sequential()


# ADD LSTM LAYER
classifier.add(LSTM(units = 10, return_sequences = True,
                    input_shape =
(X_train_3d.shape[1],X_train_3d.shape[2],)))
# LOOP WHICH ADD LSTM LAYER
for _ in range(1):
  classifier.add(LSTM(units = 10, return_sequences = True))


# LAST LSTM LAYER BUT WITH return_sequences = False
classifier.add(LSTM(units = 10, return_sequences = False))



# OUTPUT DENSE LAYER
classifier.add(Dense(1, activation="sigmoid"))


# COMPILE THE MODEL
classifier.compile(loss="binary_crossentropy", optimizer="adam")
# TRAINING
```

```
classifier.fit(X_train_3d, y_train_3d, epochs=15, batch_size=32,
verbose=1)
```

As we see, the RNN needs many resources. To avoid computation, you can take a model already trained on the internet and modify it a little bit to adapt it to your data. You also can use GPU, CPU, or TPU on Google Colab.

14.2.3. Prediction and backtest

Now that we have our algorithm, we will see the slight differences in the code when we want to make a prediction and backtest with a strategy using an RNN.

Code 14.3: Predictions and backtest

```
# Create predictions for the whole dataset
y_pred_train = np.concatenate((np.zeros([lag,1]),
classifier.predict(X_train_3d)),axis=0)
y_pred_test = np.concatenate((np.zeros([lag,1]),
classifier.predict(X_test_3d)),axis=0)

df["prediction"] = np.concatenate((y_pred_train,y_pred_test),
                                   axis=0)
df["prediction"] = np.where(df["prediction"] == 0, -1,1)

# Compute the strategy
df["strategy"] = np.sign(df["prediction"]) * df["returns"]
# Backtest
backtest_dynamic_portfolio(df["strategy"].iloc[split+lag:])
```

We need to add a vector of 0 of the lag lengths to ensure that the data will be in a good place. We have deleted 15 data each day using the function to transform the data in 3d.

As we can see on the backtest, it is an excellent algorithm because capital growth is very stable. We have excellent indicators like the Sharpe ratio of more than one, but we have a drawdown at 45%; that is why we will see in the chapter in which we are going to create the project, how we can create a portfolio of strategies to decrease the volatility of the portfolio (like previous in chapter 3 on the static portfolio optimization).

Figure 14.6: Backtest of strategy using RNN predictions on Netflix stock

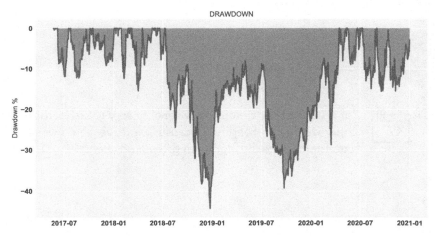

In this figure, we can see that the growth of the capital is very well, except from 2018-07 to 2019-07 with a drawdown of 45%.

14.3. RNN regressor

This section will explain how to do an RNN regressor and create a function to automate the building. To do it, we will do a tiny precision about standardization. Then we will see a new deep learning function named dropout and how to perform our trading strategy created with the RNN regressor.

14.3.1. Precision about standardization

Previously, we said that normalization should not be applied to the target. TRUE! However, using RNN, both X and y will be used to train the model. So, it will be better to normalize the y to decrease the computation time. Moreover, later we will have to do the inverse transformation on the y's afterward to get the right scale values to make our investment decisions.

Code 14.4: Standardization of the target

```
# STANDARDIZATION
sc_y = StandardScaler()
y_train_scaled = sc_y.fit_transform(y_train_reg)
y_test_scaled = sc_y.transform(y_test_reg)
```

 It is essential to create a new variable sc_y to standardize this data and keep it because we have the inverse transform once the algorithm gives predictions.

14.3. RNN regressor

14.3.2. Implementing the model

This part will explain a new concept, the dropout layer. To better utilization, we create a function RNN that allows us to create a model only taking some necessary parameters.

First, let us talk about the dropout. It is an exciting thing and very simple. It is a layer that we add to the model, which turns a percentage of the neurons of a layer off. However, why do we want to do that?

Add some dropout layer are very useful in two principal ways:

- **Better training**: Turn some neurons off and constrain the others to learn more than usual so that the model will be better trained.

- **Reduce overfitting risk**: the dropout allows us to reduce the risk of overfitting because randomly turning some neurons off forces the other neurons to not focus on one point.

Code 14.5: Factorize RNN implementation in a function

```python
def RNN(number_neurons, number_hidden_layer, shape, loss="mse",
metrics=["mae"], activation="linear", optimizer="adam",
pct_dropout=0.5):


    # LIBAIRIES
    import tensorflow
    from tensorflow.keras.models import Sequential
    from tensorflow.keras.layers import Dense, LSTM, Dropout


    # INITIALIZATION OF THE DATA
    model = Sequential()


    # ADD LSTM LAYER
    model.add(LSTM(units = number_neurons, return_sequences = True,
        input_shape = shape))


    # ADD DROPOUT LAYER
    model.add(Dropout(pct_dropout))


    # LOOP WHICH ADD LSTM AND DROPPOUT LAYER
```

```
    for _ in range(number_hidden_layer):
        model.add(LSTM(units = number_neurons, return_sequences =
True))
        model.add(Dropout(pct_dropout))


    # LAST LSTM LAYER BUT WITH return_sequences = False TO HAVE 2D
ARRAY
    model.add(LSTM(units = number_neurons, return_sequences = False))


    # ADD DROPOUT LAYER
    model.add(Dropout(pct_dropout))


    # OUTPUT DENSE LAYER
    model.add(Dense(1, activation=activation))


    # COMPILE THE MODEL
    model.compile(loss=loss, optimizer=optimizer, metrics=metrics)
    return model


regressor = RNN(15, 3, taille =
(X_train_3d.shape[1],X_train_3d.shape[2]),
                    loss = "mse", metrics=["mae"],
activation="linear",
                    optimizer="adam", pct_dropout=0.65)


regressor.fit(X_train_3d, y_train_3d, epochs=1, batch_size=32,
verbose=1)
```

14.3.3. Predictions and backtest

This part will see how to do the inverse transform of standardization and backtest the trading strategy using an RNN regressor.

Code 14.6: Inverse standardization transform and backtest

```
# Create predictions for the whole dataset
```

```
# Inverse transform

y_train_sc = sc_y.inverse_transform(regressor.predict(X_train_3d))


# Predictions

y_pred_train = np.concatenate((np.zeros([lag,1]),y_train_sc),

                                    axis=0)


# Inverse transform

y_test_sc = sc_y.inverse_transform(regressor.predict(X_test_3d))


# Predictions

y_pred_test = np.concatenate((np.zeros([lag,1]),y_test_sc),

                                   axis=0)



df["prediction"] = np.concatenate((y_pred_train,y_pred_test),

                                        axis=0)



# Compute the strategy

df["strategy"] = np.sign(df["prediction"]) * df["returns"]


# Backtest

backtest_dynamic_portfolio(df["strategy"].iloc[split+lag:])
```

As shown in figure 14.7, it is the same as for the classifier instead of
the dropout. That means that there is no overfitting in the classifier.

Figure 14.7: Backtest of strategy using RNN predictions on Netflix stock

Beta: 0.953	Alpha: 28.52 %		Sharpe: 1.04	Sortino: 1.539
VaR: 52.82 %	cVaR: 66.92 %		VaR/cVaR: 1.267	drawdown: 44.18 %

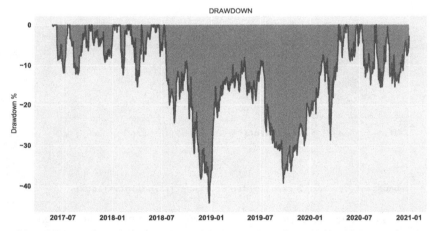

The strategy has the same returns as the classifier RNN which can be possible because it is training on the same data.

Before closing this chapter, there are some points about deep learning need to be highlighted:

- The algorithms **need many data**, nearly 50,000 or 100,000 minimum, to be trained even if we have taken a tiny database here.

- The deep learning algorithms are **the most powerful** but also the most challenging to train because of the number of hyperparameters.

- **The risk of overfitting** increases with the number of parameters. So, neural networks are very touched by these issues.

Summary

- The data need to be 3-dimensional to train an RNN because each observation is a 2-dimensional matrix.

- The Recurrent neural network is useful when we work on time series.

- The dropout layer allows us to turn some neural off to optimize the training and avoid overfitting.

Application Live Trading and Screener
This code is based on the class created in the annex: MetaTrader

Code 14.7: Application Trading / RNN Regressor

```
from MT5 import *

import numpy as np

import pandas as pd

import warnings

warnings.filterwarnings("ignore")

import time

import pickle

from joblib import dump, load

import os

from sklearn.preprocessing import StandardScaler

from tensorflow.keras.models import Sequential

from tensorflow.keras.layers import Dense, LSTM, Dropout


path = "" # Ex: C:/Desktop/Python_for_finance_and_algorithmic_trading/
ChapterN/


def X_3d_RNN(X_s, y_s, lag):
```

```python
        # Simple verification
        if len(X_s) != len(y_s):
            print("Warnings")


        # Create the X_train
        X_train = []
        for variable in range(0, X_s.shape[1]):
            X = []
            for i in range(lag, X_s.shape[0]):
                X.append(X_s[i-lag:i, variable])
            X_train.append(X)
        X_train, np.array(X_train)
        X_train = np.swapaxes(np.swapaxes(X_train, 0, 1), 1, 2)


        # Create the y_train
        y_train = []
        for i in range(lag, y_s.shape[0]):
            y_train.append(y_s[i, :].reshape(-1,1).transpose())
        y_train = np.concatenate(y_train, axis=0)
        return X_train, y_train



def RNN():
        # Create the model
        number_hidden_layer = 15
        number_neurons = 10
        loss="mse"
        metrics=["mae"]
        activation="linear"
        optimizer="adam"
        pct_dropout=0.5


      # INITIALIZATION OF THE DATA
      model = Sequential()


      # ADD LSTM LAYER
```

```python
    model.add(LSTM(units  =  number_neurons,  return_sequences  =  True,
input_shape = (15,5,)))

    # ADD DROPOUT LAYER
    model.add(Dropout(pct_dropout))

    # LOOP WHICH ADD LSTM AND DROPPOUT LAYER
    for _ in range(number_hidden_layer):
        model.add(LSTM(units = number_neurons, return_sequences = True))
        model.add(Dropout(pct_dropout))

    # LAST LSTM LAYER BUT WITH return_sequences = False
    model.add(LSTM(units = number_neurons, return_sequences = False))

    # ADD DROPOUT LAYER
    model.add(Dropout(pct_dropout))

    # OUTPUT DENSE LAYER
    model.add(Dense(1, activation=activation))

    # COMPILE THE MODEL
    model.compile(loss=loss, optimizer=optimizer, metrics=metrics)
    return model

def create_model_weights(symbol):
    """ Weights for Linear regression on the percentage change"""
    # Import the data
    data = MT5.get_data(symbol, 3500)[["close"]].pct_change(1)

    # Create new variable
    data.columns = ["returns"]

    # Features engeeniring
    data["returns t-1"] = data[["returns"]].shift(1)

    # Mean of returns
    data["mean returns 15"] = data[["returns"]].rolling(15).mean()
.shift(1)
```

267

```
    data["mean returns 60"] = data[["returns"]].rolling(60).mean()
.shift(1)


    # Volatility of returns
    data["volatility returns 15"] = data[["returns"]].rolling(15).std()
.shift(1)
    data["volatility returns 60"] = data[["returns"]].rolling(60).std()
.shift(1)


    # Split the data
    data = data.dropna()
    split = int(0.80*len(data))


    # Train set creation
    X_train = data[["returns t-1", "mean returns 15", "mean returns 60",
              "volatility returns 15",
              "volatility returns 60"]].iloc[:split]
    y_train = np.round(data[["returns"]].iloc[:split]+0.5)




    # Initialize the class
    sc = StandardScaler()


    # Standardize the data
    X_train = sc.fit_transform(X_train)


    lag = 15
    X_train, y_train = X_3d_RNN(X_train, y_train.values, 15)


    alg = RNN()


    # TRAINING
    alg.fit(X_train, y_train, epochs=1, batch_size=32, verbose=1)


    # Save the model
    print("Train the model because there are no existed weights")
    alg.save_weights(os.path.join(path,f"Models/RNN_reg_{symbol}"))
```

```python
def RNN_reg_sig(symbol):
    """ Function for predict the value of tommorow using ARIMA model"""

    # Create the weights if there is not in the folder
    try:
        alg = RNN()
        alg.load_weights(os.path.join(path,f"Models/RNN_reg_{symbol}"))
    except:
        create_model_weights(symbol)
        alg = RNN()
        alg.load_weights(os.path.join(path,f"Models/RNN_reg_{symbol}"))

    # Take the lastest percentage of change
    data = MT5.get_data(symbol, 3500)[["close"]].pct_change(1)
    # Create new variable
    data.columns = ["returns"]

    # Features engeeniring
    data["returns t-1"] = data[["returns"]].shift(1)

    # Mean of returns
    data["mean returns 15"] = data[["returns"]].rolling(15).mean()
.shift(1)
    data["mean returns 60"] = data[["returns"]].rolling(60).mean()
.shift(1)

    # Volatility of returns
    data["volatility returns 15"] = data[["returns"]].rolling(15).std()
.shift(1)
    data["volatility returns 60"] = data[["returns"]].rolling(60).std()
.shift(1)


    X = data[["returns t-1", "mean returns 15", "mean returns 60",
            "volatility returns 15",
```

269

```
            "volatility returns 60"]]


    # Initialize the class
    sc = StandardScaler()


    # Standardize the data
    X = sc.fit_transform(X)


    y = data[["returns t-1"]]


    X, _ = X_3d_RNN(X, y.values, 15)


    X = X[-1:,:,:]


    # Find the signal
    prediction = alg.predict(X)
    buy = prediction[0][0] > 0
    sell =not buy



    return buy, sell




# True = Live Trading and Flse = Screener
live = True



if live:
    current_account_info = mt5.account_info()
    print("-----------------------------------------------------------")
    print("Date: ", datetime.now().strftime("%Y-%m-%d %H:%M:%S"))
    print(f"Balance: {current_account_info.balance} USD, \t"
          f"Equity: {current_account_info.equity} USD, \t"
          f"Profit: {current_account_info.profit} USD")
    print("-----------------------------------------------------------")
```

```python
info_order = {

    "Netflix": ["Netflix_Inc_(NFLX.O)", 1.00]

}



start = datetime.now().strftime("%H:%M:%S")#"23:59:59"
while True:
    # Verfication for launch
    if datetime.now().weekday() not in (5,1):
        is_time = datetime.now().strftime("%H:%M:%S") == start
    else:
        is_time = False



    # Launch the algorithm
    if is_time:

        # Open the trades
        for asset in info_order.keys():

            # Initialize the inputs
            symbol = info_order[asset][0]
            lot = info_order[asset][1]

            # Create the signals
            buy, sell = RNN_reg_sig(symbol)

             # Run the algorithm
            if live:
                MT5.run(symbol, buy, sell,lot)

            else:
                print(f"Symbol: {symbol}\t"
                    f"Buy: {buy}\t"
                    f"Sell: {sell}")
    time.sleep(1)
```

The live parameter sets the live trading (live = True) or the screener mode (live = False).

Chapter 15: Bonus / Example of RNN with CNN (RCNN)

In this bonus, we will an example of an advanced deep learning algorithm, the RCNN, which combines a 1d-CNN[17] and an RNN. It allows us to keep the best of the two models.

Indeed, the RNN is good for finding relationships in time because it is a time series analysis algorithm. At the same time, CNN can catch more features because it has a different method to fit.

15.1. Intuition of CNN

The Convolutional neural network (CNN) specialty is that it works with filters. The filters in a CNN layer are like the number of neurons with an RNN. The more filters there are, the more the algorithm is complex. CNN is mainly used for image detection. We will explain a little bit the notion using the example of an image.

Figure 15.1: Intuition behind CNN

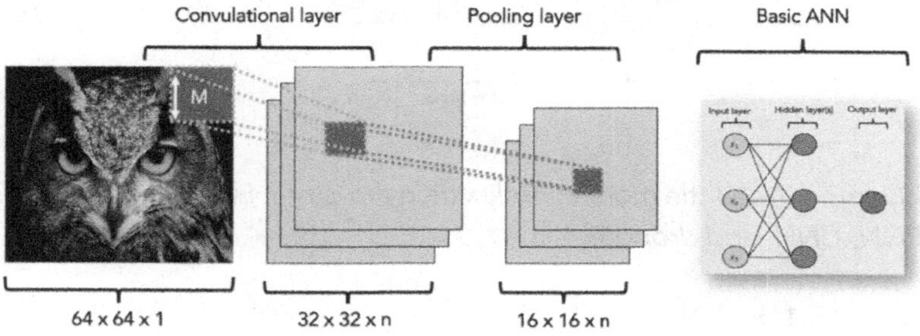

In this figure, we can see the representation of CNN's functioning.

- M is the length of the stripe, which is a significant parameter. If the stripe is too tiny, our algorithm takes too much time to train, increasing the overfitting risk. Do not forget that the more your increase the complexity, the more the overfitting risk increase.

---

[17] **Additional lecture**: Introduction to Convolutional Neural Networks (CNN), Manav Mandal

- N is the number of filters. The more filters there are, the more powerful and take time to train.

- The convolutional layer is created by the function conv1D or conv2D of TensorFlow.

- The pooling layer allows us to reduce the shape, whereas we will not use it in our model.

15.2. Create an RCNN

Each neural network has many structures, particularly this one, because it combines them. We will use a 1-dimensional CNN because it needs 3-dimensional data like the RNN.

Figure 15.2: Description of the model

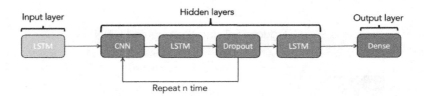

Our model is a little more complex than the other. Indeed, it combines RNN, CNN, and dropout.

Code 15.1: RCNN

```
def RCNN(number_neurons, number_hidden_layer, shape, loss="mse",
metrics=["mae"], activation="linear", optimizer="adam",
pct_dropout=0.5):


  # LIBAIRIES
  import tensorflow
  from tensorflow.keras.models import Sequential
  from tensorflow.keras.layers import Conv1D, Dense, LSTM, Dropout


  # INITIALIZATION OF THE DATA
```

274

```python
    model = Sequential()

    # ADD LSTM LAYER
    model.add(LSTM(units = number_neurons, return_sequences = True,
input_shape = shape))

    # ADD DROPOUT LAYER
    model.add(Dropout(pct_dropout))

    # LOOP WHICH ADD LSTM AND DROPPOUT LAYER
    for _ in range(number_hidden_layer):
      model.add(Conv1D(64,3, activation='relu'))
      model.add(LSTM(units = number_neurons, return_sequences =
True))
      model.add(Dropout(pct_dropout))

    # LAST LSTM LAYER BUT WITH return_sequences = False
    model.add(LSTM(units = number_neurons, return_sequences = False))

    # OUTPUT DENSE LAYER
    model.add(Dense(1, activation=activation))

    # COMPILE THE MODEL
    model.compile(loss=loss, optimizer=optimizer, metrics=metrics)
    return model

regressor = RNN(15, 3, shape =
(X_train_3d.shape[1],X_train_3d.shape[2]),
                loss = "mse", metrics=["mae"],
activation="linear",
                optimizer="adam", pct_dropout=0.65)

regressor.fit(X_train_3d, y_train_3d, epochs=1, batch_size=32,
verbose=1)
```

15.3. Backtest

In this section, we will backtest the trading strategy based on an RCNN. For that we will use the same function as previously created in chapter 5.

Figure 15.3: Backtest of the strategy using RCNN Google predictions

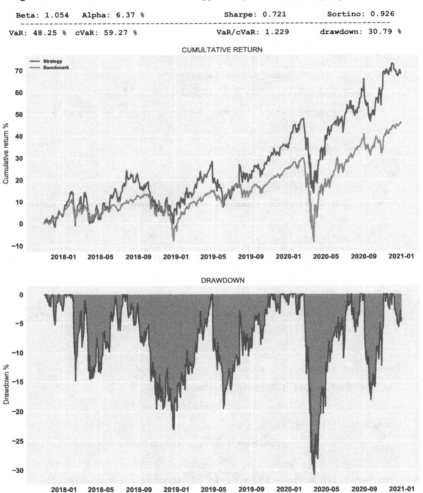

The strategy is good because the alpha, Sharpe, and Sortino ratios are positive. The beta is close to 1, which means we correlate to the market returns. The drawdown is close to 30%, which is high but good for a strategy without combining other strategies.

Chapter 16: Real-life full project

In the previous chapter, we have seen a lot of techniques and algorithms from many fields. We will see that to put a robust quantitative trading algorithm in place, the key is using all these fields simultaneously to take advantage of each. We will combine machine learning to create predictive algorithms, statistics to do features engineering, and portfolio management to combine our strategies to decrease the risk of this investment.

First, we will search for many assets for our strategy. Then we will select the best assets using a Sharpe ratio criterion. Moreover, we will find the optimal stop loss, take profit, and leverage.

16.1. Preparation of the data

In all projects in finance, the data are the most important thing. The most powerful algorithm cannot predict if we ask it to predict Google stock price using the ice cream consummation. It is exaggerated, but we need to prepare the data with the most attention we can because we can lose money by one error into them. Usually, the data preparation is 60 to 80% of the project.

16.1.1. Import the data

The goal of the strategy is to test some algorithms on many assets. The point is that we already know how to import data using a symbol. So, why is there a part to explain that? We want to work with all the assets available on our broker. There are more than 2000. Thus, we need to run a little code to have all of them.

Moreover, we will work with the data of our broker directly because we need to be as close as possible to the market. Indeed, in the previous chapter, we explored each technique using Yahoo data. Indeed, the point was to explain that the techniques do not create a strategy in the previous chapters. However, when we work on a real-life project, it is better to have the broker data using the MetaTrader 5 platform because it is closer to reality.

Code 16.1: How scrap all the symbol name

```
# INITIALIZE THE DEVICE
mt5.initialize()


# Create empty list
symbols = []
sectors = []
descriptions = []


# Get the information for all symbol
symbols_information = mt5.symbols_get() 1


# Tuple to list
symbols_information_list = list(symbols_information) 2


# Extract the name of the symbol
for element in symbols_information_list:
    symbols.append(list(element)[-3]) 3
    sectors.append(list(element)[-1].split("\\")[0]) 4
    descriptions.append(list(element)[-7]) 5


# Create a dataframe
informations = pd.DataFrame([symbols, sectors, descriptions],
index=["Symbol", "Sector", "Description"]).transpose() 6
```

1   The function symbols_get() give us the information for all the symbols the broker offers us to trade.

2   symbols_get() return a tuple, so we need to transform it into a list to work with this object.

3   Take the symbol of the asset.

4   Take the path to have the sector of the asset.

5   Take a description of the asset.

6   Put all information into a dataframe.

Figure 16.1: Extraction of the symbols and their sector

Symbol	Sector	Description
AUDUSD	FX Majors	Australian Vs US
EURUSD	FX Majors	US Vs Euro

We can see that we have scrapped all the symbols with its sector. Thus, it is easy to do if we want to try an algorithm only on one sector.

 Selecting a sector can be interesting if we create an algorithm that uses bagging on assets.

Our strategy will take only the assets with a meager spread. It is a personal choice. We can choose another criterion of asset selection, such as the volatility of the asset.

Code 16.2: Find the lowest spread asset

```
# Create empty list
spread = []


# Computze the spread
for symbol in informations["Symbol"]:
    try:
        ask =  mt5.symbol_info_tick(symbol).ask
        bid =  mt5.symbol_info_tick(symbol).bid
        spread.append((ask - bid) / ask )
    except:
        spread.append(None)


# Take the assets with the spread < 0.07%
informations["Spread"] = spread
lowest_spread_asset = informations.dropna().\
```

```
loc[informations["Spread"]<0.0007]
```

16.1.2. Features engineering

As said previously, the data are an essential part of the project. Thus, we cannot give the algorithm only the OHLC data because it is insufficient. We need to help our algorithm. To do it, we will use the previous features' engineering method. Indeed, we will create some moving averages and some moving volatility in the function. Then, we will apply a PCA algorithm to the dataset to reduce the number of columns.

Code 16.3: Create new features and apply PCA

```python
def features_engeeniring(df):
    """ This function which creates all the necessary sets for the
    algorithms"""


    # Allows the variables to be call outside the function
    global X_train
    global X_test
    global y_train_reg
    global y_train_cla
    global X_train_scaled
    global X_test_scaled
    global split_train_test
    global split_test_valid
    global X_valid
    global X_valid_scaled
    global X_train_pca
    global X_test_pca
    global X_val_pca


    # Create ours own metrics to compute the strategy returns
    df["returns"] = ((df["close"] - df["close"].shift(1)) / df["close"])
```

280

```
.shift(1)
    df["sLow"] = ((df["low"] - df["close"].shift(1)) / df["close"]
.shift(1)).shift(1)
    df["sHigh"] = ((df["high"] - df["close"].shift(1)) / df["close"]
.shift(1)).shift(1)


    # Features engineering
    df["returns t-1"] = df[["returns"]].shift(1)


    # Mean of returns
    df["mean returns 15"] = df[["returns"]].rolling(15).mean().shift(1)
    df["mean returns 60"] = df[["returns"]].rolling(60).mean().shift(1)


    # Volatility of returns
    df["volatility returns 15"] = df[["returns"]].rolling(15).std()
.shift(1)
    df["volatility returns 60"] = df[["returns"]].rolling(60).std()
.shift(1)


    # Drop missing values
    df = df.dropna()


    # Percentage train set
    split = int(0.80*len(df))


    list_x = ["returns t-1", "mean returns 15", "mean returns 60",
                "volatility returns 15",
                "volatility returns 60"]


    split_train_test = int(0.70*len(df))
    split_test_valid = int(0.90*len(df))


    # Train set creation
    X_train = df[list_x].iloc[:split_train_test]


    y_train_reg = df[["returns"]].iloc[:split_train_test]
```

```
y_train_cla = np.round(df[["returns"]].iloc[:split_train_test]+0.5)



# Test set creation
X_test = df[list_x].iloc[split_train_test:split_test_valid]


# Test set creation
X_val = df[list_x].iloc[split_test_valid:]



# NORMALIZATION
# Import the class
from sklearn.preprocessing import StandardScaler


# Initialize the class
sc = StandardScaler()


# Standardize the data
X_train_scaled = sc.fit_transform(X_train)

X_test_scaled = sc.transform(X_test)

X_val_scaled = sc.transform(X_val)



# PCA
# Import the class
from sklearn.decomposition import PCA


# Initiliaze the class
pca = PCA(n_components=3)


# Apply the PCA
X_train_pca = pca.fit_transform(X_train_scaled)

X_test_pca = pca.transform(X_test_scaled)

X_val_pca = pca.transform(X_val_scaled)
```

If the function modifies the values of the global variable, then it must be declared by preceding it with the keyword global.

In the next section, we will train all algorithms with the same data, as in chapter 10. It is better to train different models with different (independent) features to have better results. So, in your project, you can find the best features for each asset, but it takes a lot of time.

16.1.3. Train, test and validation sets

In the previous chapters, to test the performances of our algorithms, we have used the train set to train the algorithm and the test set to test its performance. In a more significant project, we need to create three sets of data: the train set, the test set, and the validation set.

This project must have three sets because we work with predictive models, and we need one set to train it and two sets to work with portfolio management technics. Let us see in figure 14.3 the utility of each set in our project.

- **Training set:** It allows us to train the predictive models. We do not train the optimal portfolio allocation with the train set because the predictions on the train set are not significant (because the algorithm already knows the data because it is fit to them).

- **Test set:** It allows us to find the best predictive models on the unknown data. Then, because the returns of the strategy based on the predictions are significant here (because the algorithm does not know the data before), we choose the bests models (with the criterion of your choice). Then, we have our best models. We can find the optimal portfolio allocation between our n best strategies (only on the test set returns).

- **Validation set:** Now, we have the best models and the best allocation of our capital between the models (the best portfolio allocation). We can backtest the portfolio on this anonymous data.

Figure 16.2: Utility of each set of data

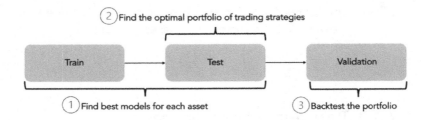

We can see a little summary of the decision process to find the best portfolio of trading strategies.

16.2. Modelling the strategy

We have prepared many functions for the data: import, feature engineering and transformation. This section aims to find assets with a low spread that are not subject to the weak efficiency market.

First, we will find the bests strategies using a Sharpe ratio criterion. Then, we will take the most profitable strategies and use a voting method on the algorithm. Moreover, we will use a portfolio method on the test set data to find the best allocation in our portfolio strategies.

16.2.1. Find the best assets

We will take the symbols with a spread lower than our spread threshold of 0.07%.

Then, we will compute the Sharpe ratio of a trading strategy created using each machine learning algorithm. Furthermore, we take the strategy with the highest Sharpe ratio. We will use only classifier algorithms for this project, but we can use regression algorithms in our project. It is the same.

 We cannot work with deep learning algorithms for this project because some assets have only 1000 data. So, we need to use the appropriate algorithms: linear regression, SVR, and decision tree.

First, to automate the functioning, we need to create a function that produces a strategy and compute the Sharpe ratio of this strategy on the test set. The only required parameter is the model that we want to use. If we are going to test a regression algorithm, we have to use the parameter reg=True.

Code 16.4: Predictor function

```python
def predictor(model, reg=True, spread=0.035):
    global df
    model.fit(X_train, y_train_cla)



    df = df.dropna()
    # Create predictions for the whole dataset
    df["prediction"] = model.predict(np.concatenate((X_train,
X_test, X_valid), axis=0))
    if reg==False:
        df["prediction"] = np.where(df["prediction"]==0, -1, 1)
    # Compute the strategy
    df["strategy"] = np.sign(df["prediction"]) * df["returns"]
```

```
    returns =
df["strategy"].iloc[split_train_test:split_test_valid]


    return np.sqrt(252) * (returns.mean()~(spread/100))/
returns.std()
```

We add the spread of the asset in the computation of the Sharpe ratio because all the assets do not have the same spread. So, the more the asset spread is significant, the more it will be penalized.

Keep attention to the spread, sometimes it is in percentage and sometimes not. Thus, verify before using it.

With this function, we can automate the computation of 450 trading strategies. Indeed, we will take 150 assets, and we will try 3 machine learning algorithms.

Code 16.5: Automatization of the testing

```
# Import the class
from sklearn.svm import SVR
from sklearn.tree import DecisionTreeRegressor
from sklearn.linear_model import LinearRegression


from tqdm import tqdm
# Models
tree = DecisionTreeRegressor(max_depth=6)
svr = SVR(epsilon=1.5)
lin = LinearRegression()



# Initialization
symbols = symbols[:150]#["EURUSD", "GBPAUD"]
lists = []


for symbol in tqdm(symbols):
    try:
```

```
        df = data(symbol,
3500)[["close"]].dropna().pct_change(1).dropna()
        df.columns = ["returns"]
        features_engeeniring(df)


        """ Decision tree rgressor"""
        sharpe_tree = predictor(tree, reg=True)
        lists.append([symbol, "Tree", sharpe_tree])



        """ SVR """
        sharpe_svr = predictor(svr, reg=True)
        lists.append([symbol, "SVR", sharpe_svr])


        """ Linear Regression"""
        sharpe_linreg = predictor(lin, reg=True)
        lists.append([symbol, "LinReg", sharpe_linreg])
    except:
        pass
```

With this code, we have found the Sharpe ratio for each strategy. We will take the asset with the best Sharpe ratio and have good results with the three algorithms.

The three algorithms chosen are very different. The linear regression finds linear patterns, the SVR the non-linear, and the decision tree also has another way to fit it. So, if these three algorithms have good results, we optimize our chances of better results.

Figure 16.3: Bests assets chosen

Asset	Bitcoin	JPN225	NAS100	US2000	XPTUSD
Sortino	2.9	1.6	1.2	1.1	0.7

This table shows the best assets of our selection with their Sortino ratio compute on the test set.

287

16.2.2. Combine the algorithms

In chapter 10, we have seen the power of the ensemble method. Here, we will apply the voting method. This method will combine the three previous algorithms: decision tree, SVC, and Logistic regression.

We have seven assets with an excellent Sharpe ratio on the test set. Before creating a portfolio using these strategies, we need to create one algorithm to predict each asset. To do it, we will use a voting classifier.

Code 16.6: Voting classifier implementation

```
def voting(df, reg=True):
        """ Create a strategy using a voting method"""
        # Import the class


        # Import the models
        if reg:
            tree = DecisionTreeRegressor(max_depth=6)
            svr = SVR(epsilon=1.5)
            lin = LinearRegression()
            vot = VotingRegressor(estimators=[
                ('lr', lin), ("tree", tree), ("svr", svr)])
        else:
            tree = DecisionTreeClassifier(max_depth=6)
            svr = SVC()
            lin = LogisticRegression()

            vot = VotingClassifier(estimators=[
                ('lr', lin), ("tree", tree), ("svr", svr)])

        # Train the model
        if reg==False:
            vot.fit(X_train_pca, y_train_cla)
        else:
            vot.fit(X_train_pca, y_train_reg)
```

```
# Remove missing values
df = df.dropna()


# Create predictions for the whole dataset
df["prediction"] = vot.predict(np.concatenate((X_train_pca,
                                                X_test_pca,
                                                X_val_pca),
                                    axis=0))


# Remove missing values
df = df.dropna()


if reg==False:
    df["prediction"] = np.where(df["prediction"]==0, -1, 1)


# Compute the strategy
df["strategy"] = np.sign(df["prediction"]).shift(1) *
df["returns"]
    df["low_strategy"] = np.where(df["prediction"]>0, df["sLow"], -
df["sHigh"])
    df["high_strategy"] = np.where(df["prediction"]>0, df["sHigh"],
-df["sLow"])



    return     vot,     df["strategy"],     df["low_strategy"],
df["high_strategy"]
```

 We also return the voting model to save it in a folder for the live trading algorithm implementation (Annex: How to save a model in scikit-learn and Tensorflow).

As we can see in figure 16.4, the return of each asset alone is not very profitable, taking into account the volatility of these strategies. The following subsection will apply a portfolio method to the trading strategies to decrease the investment risk.

Figure 16.4.: Cumulative returns of the portfolio assets on the test set

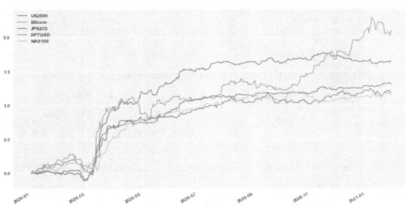

This figure shows the cumulative return of each asset of the portfolio. As we can see, the strategies are not very profitable and very risky alone.

16.2.3. Apply portfolio management technics

We have seven strategies for trading, and we will use portfolio management techniques to create a portfolio to work with as one strategy in the following section. Furthermore, we will use the mean-variance-skewness-kurtosis criterion because it allows us to have a less risky portfolio.

Figure 16.5: Backtest of the portfolio on the test set

```
Beta:    -0.144   Alpha: 27.36 %   Sharpe:   0.603   Sortino: 0.954
-----------------------------------------------------------------------
VaR: 66.69 %   cVaR:    79.23 %   VaR/cVaR: 1.188   drawdown: 20.91 %
```

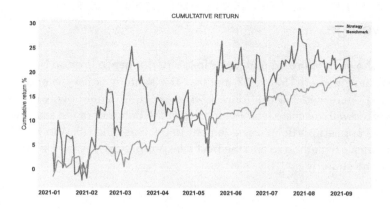

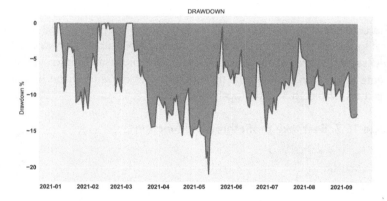

This figure shows us the backtest of the portfolio without leverage, stop loss or take profit. As we can see, the backtest is good, with an alpha of 27%. There is a good trend in the profit but with high volatility.

The allocation of the portfolio is to remove two assets. Thus, we take 31% of our budget of Russel 2000, 50% of Bitcoin, and 19% of JPN 225. The criterion considers that the other assets are too risky or not enough profitable to come into the portfolio. Moreover, the drawdown remains high because the majority of the underlying assets are very volatile.

16.3. Find optimal take profit, stop loss and leverage

As shown in figure 16.6, the portfolio's performance is good because we have earned 15% in 12 months. The strategy is risky even if we have decreased the risk (drawdown max: 20%). Until now, we have worked with machine learning to predict the behavior of the asset. We have applied portfolio management to decrease the risk. We will use a statistical method to find the best take profit, stop loss, and leverage for the strategy.

16.3.1. Optimal take profit (tp)

The take profit threshold of a strategy is critical. It can change a non-profitable strategy into a profitable strategy. This subsection will see a grid search technique to find the best take profit threshold. We will create a function that returns the Sharpe ratio depending on his take profit threshold to find the optimal values.

Code 16.7: Best take profit threshold function

```python
def find_best_tp(tp):

    tp = tp/100


    # Create the portfolio
    pf = pd.concat((low_portfolio, portfolio_return_test,
high_portfolio), axis=1).dropna()-spread


    pf.columns = ["low", "Return", "high"]


    # Apply the tp
    pf["Return"] = np.where(pf["high"].values>tp, tp,
pf["Return"].values)
    pf["Return"] = np.where(pf["Return"].values>tp, tp,
pf["Return"].values)


    # Return sharpe raatio
    return np.sqrt(252)*pf["Return"].mean()/pf["Return"].std()
```

```
pd.DataFrame([find_best_tp(tp) for tp in np.linspace(1.5,3,10)],
index=np.linspace(1.5,3,10), columns=["Sharpe"])
```

 We replace return by the take profit when the high of the day is above the tp threshold. We do the same for the returns because sometimes, in real life, there are issues in the data (high < close, for example).

 Using this function, we will converge to a tp of 0. However, the best profit threshold does not consider the swap, a penalty, or a bonus given by the broker to incite people to go in a certain way. If the tp is very low in the backtest, you will have a profitable strategy, but the swap will take all your profit in real life. It is necessary to keep a high enough take profit threshold.

With our computation, we have found an optimal take profit threshold at 2.1% on the test set with a Sharpe ratio of 3.7 on the validation period but less in real life because there are additional fees that we cannot consider precisely. Thus, 40% in 9 months of the validation period does not mean we need to put in production with 100 000$ now. **We need to put in a demo account to find the real-life best parameters for our strategies and ensure there are no issues in our computations.**

16.3.2. Optimal stop loss (sl)

Previously, we have seen how to earn money, but the stop loss's utility is to avoid losing money. In this subsection, we will only create a strategy with a stop loss because we cannot combine tp and sl with the daily data (confer chapter 6). Indeed, we cannot say which threshold is passed first.

Using the find_best_sl function, we are going to find the best sl. Moreover, we will see a convergence of the Sharpe ratio after 9.6% of sl. It means that there are no values after this point. Thus, we can put this threshold in our strategy because we need an sl in trading, and this threshold is never touched in the test set.

Code 16.7: find best stop loss threshold

```python
def find_best_sl(sl):

    sl = sl/100


    # Create the portfolio
    pf = pd.concat((low_portfolio, portfolio_return_test,
                    high_portfolio),axis=1).dropna()-spread
    pf.columns = ["low", "Return", "high"]


    # Apply the sl
    pf["Return"] = np.where(pf["low"].values<-sl, -sl,
pf["Return"].values)
    pf["Return"] = np.where(pf["Return"].values<-sl, -sl,
                                        pf["Return"].values)


    # Return sharpe raatio
    return np.sqrt(252)*pf["Return"].mean()/pf["Return"].std()


pd.DataFrame([find_best_sl(sl) for sl in np.linspace(3,10,30)],
             index=np.linspace(3,10,30), columns=["Sharpe"])
```

So, we have a tp at 2.1% and an sl at 9.6% for our strategy. It only misses leverage to optimize the earn of the strategy.

16.3.3. Optimal leverage

Leverage multiplies our investment power and our profits. However, it also multiplies our risk in the same way. If we are new to trading, we must master this tool and understand how to use it effectively.

Depending on our level of risk aversion, there are several ways to determine the best leverage to use. One of the best known is the Kelly criterion.
We will use another method: the drawdown method. In finance, all people are unique, so it cannot be one method to find the best leverage because it depends on the risk aversion of each investor.

The drawdown method is straightforward to compute, we take the max drawdown of our strategy without leverage (Md_1), and we must know the maximum drawdown we want ($Md_{leverage}$). Then leverage is:

$$leverage = \frac{Md_{leverage}}{Md_1}$$

So, suppose we work with our strategy using 2.1% for the tp threshold and 9% for the sl. In that case, we want a maximum drawdown of 15% because we are not risky lovers, and the maximum drawdown is 10%. Then the leverage for the strategy is 15/10 = 1.5.

We have all the financial hyperparameters of the strategy. A take profit threshold at 2.1%, stop loss threshold at 9%, and optimal leverage at 1.5

Figure 16.6: Backtest the portfolio with leverage, sl and tp

```
  Beta: -0.174    Alpha: 93.37 %.   Sharpe: 2.178      Sortino: 2.529
-------------------------------------------------------------------------
  VaR: 5.95 %.    cVaR: 20.88 %     VaR/cVaR: 3.508    drawdown: 13.32 %
```

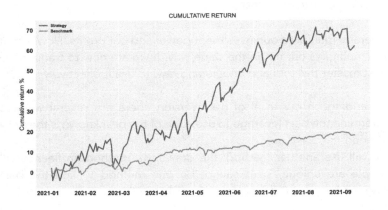

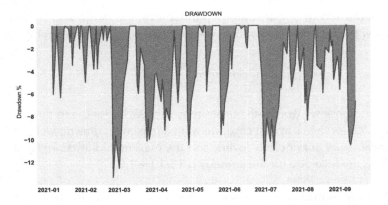

How to improve the project?

- Use ticks to do the backtest to find better combinations between taking profit and stop-loss threshold.

- Use ticks to compute the spread in the time and not at one day to select the asset because it is not representative.

- Use ticks to work with subsequent stop loss.

- Try to use bagging on assets in a deep learning algorithm.

- Try another criterion than the spread to select assets.

- Adjust the leverage depending on the calculation of the interest

- Trailing stop loss to optimize the gain

Application Live Trading and Screener

This code is based on the class created in the annex: MetaTrader

Code 16.6: Application Trading / Project

```python
from MT5 import *

import numpy as np

import pandas as pd

import warnings

warnings.filterwarnings("ignore")

from sklearn.svm import SVC

from sklearn.tree import DecisionTreeClassifier

from sklearn.linear_model import LogisticRegression

import time

from sklearn.ensemble import VotingClassifier

import pickle

from joblib import dump, load

import os

from sklearn.preprocessing import StandardScaler


path = "" # Ex: C:/Desktop/Python_for_finance_and_algorithmic_trading/
ChapterN/



def create_model_weights(symbol):
    """ Weights for Linear regression on the percentage change"""
    # Import the data
    data = MT5.get_data(symbol, 3500)[["close"]].pct_change(1)


    # Create new variable
    data.columns = ["returns"]


    # Features engeeniring
```

```
    data["returns t-1"] = data[["returns"]].shift(1)


    # Mean of returns
    data["mean returns 15"] = data[["returns"]].rolling(15).mean()
.shift(1)
    data["mean returns 60"] = data[["returns"]].rolling(60).mean()
.shift(1)


    # Volatility of returns
    data["volatility returns 15"] = data[["returns"]].rolling(15).std()
.shift(1)
    data["volatility returns 60"] = data[["returns"]].rolling(60).std()
.shift(1)


    # Split the data
    data = data.dropna()
    split = int(0.80*len(data))


    # Train set creation
    X_train = data[["returns t-1", "mean returns 15", "mean returns 60",
            "volatility returns 15",
            "volatility returns 60"]].iloc[:split]
    y_train = np.round(data[["returns"]].iloc[:split]+0.5)


    sc = StandardScaler()
    X_train = sc.fit_transform(X_train)


    # Create the model
    tree = DecisionTreeClassifier(max_depth=6)
    svr = SVC()
    lin = LogisticRegression()


    alg = VotingClassifier(estimators=[
        ('lr', lin), ("tree", tree), ("svr", svr)])


    # Fit the model
    alg.fit(X_train, y_train)
```

```python
    # Save the model
    alg_var = pickle.dumps(alg)

    alg_pickel = pickle.loads(alg_var)


    dump(alg_pickel ,os.path.join(path,f"Models/{symbol}_reg.joblib"))



def vot_cla_sig(symbol):
    """ Function for predict the value of tommorow using ARIMA model"""


    # Create the weights if there is not in the folder
    try:
        alg = load(os.path.join(path,f"Models/{symbol}_reg.joblib"))
    except:
        create_model_weights(symbol)
        alg = load(os.path.join(path,f"Models/{symbol}_reg.joblib"))


    # Take the lastest percentage of change
    data = MT5.get_data(symbol, 3500)[["close"]].pct_change(1)


    # Create new variable
    data.columns = ["returns"]


    # Features engeeniring
    data["returns t-1"] = data[["returns"]].shift(1)


    # Mean of returns
    data["mean returns 15"] = data[["returns"]].rolling(15).mean()
.shift(1)
    data["mean returns 60"] = data[["returns"]].rolling(60).mean()
.shift(1)


    # Volatility of returns
    data["volatility returns 15"] = data[["returns"]].rolling(15).std()
.shift(1)
    data["volatility returns 60"] = data[["returns"]].rolling(60).std()
.shift(1)
```

```python
    X = data[["returns t-1", "mean returns 15", "mean returns 60",
              "volatility returns 15",
              "volatility returns 60"]].iloc[-1:,:].values


    # Find the signal
    prediction = alg.predict(X)
    prediction = np.where(prediction==0, -1, 1)
    buy = prediction[0] > 0
    sell = not buy



    return buy, sell



# True = Live Trading and False = Screener
live = True

if live:
    current_account_info = mt5.account_info()
    print("-------------------------------------------------------------")
    print("Date: ", datetime.now().strftime("%Y-%m-%d %H:%M:%S"))
    print(f"Balance: {current_account_info.balance} USD, \t"
          f"Equity: {current_account_info.equity} USD, \t"
          f"Profit: {current_account_info.profit} USD")
    print("-------------------------------------------------------------



info_order = {
    "RUSSEL 2000": ["US2000", 1.1],
    "Bitcoin": ["Bitcoin", 0.1],
    "Nasdaq 100": ["NAS100", 0.3]
}



start = datetime.now().strftime("%H:%M:%S")
while True:
    # Verfication for launch
    if datetime.now().weekday() not in (5,3):
```

```python
        is_time    =    datetime.now().strftime("%H:%M:%S")    ==    start
#"23:59:59"
    else:
        is_time = False



    # Launch the algorithm
    if is_time:

        # Open the trades
        for asset in info_order.keys():

            # Initialize the inputs
            symbol = info_order[asset][0]
            lot = info_order[asset][1]

            # Create the signals
            buy, sell = vot_cla_sig(symbol)

             # Run the algorithm
            if live:
                MT5.run(symbol, buy, sell,lot)

            else:
                print(f"Symbol: {symbol}\t"
                      f"Buy: {buy}\t"
                      f"Sell: {sell}")
        time.sleep(1)
```

Chapter 17: From nothing to live trading

This chapter discusses the process of creating and putting a trading strategy into production, managing a live trading strategy, and combining strategies between them.

17.1 Trading strategies creation guidelines

This section will first recap the whole process to create a trading strategy properly to minimize the risk of error. Then we will discuss the trading plan and trading journal.

17.1.1 The trading plan

Many people neglect the trading plan but remember that many people also lose money. It is not a perfect relationship, but a negative relationship exists between making a trading plan and being profitable. Why? Because the trading plan is created with a fresh mind before beginning manual trading. So, it will be easier to follow the plan if we have our guidelines when searching for more than 50 hours for a profitable trading strategy. Because modifying the trading plan according to difficulties is not good.

As we are not making manual trading here, the trading plan will be slightly different, as we already know. A trading plan will give us the entry and exit point with the money management to follow for each strategy. However, if we have automatized this, we do not need to check it for each trade. So, in algo trading, what a trading plan looks like?
We need to put all the strategy characteristics in the same place, i.e., the performance, the risk, how many trades we want to take (maximum one trade and at least three trades in a day), which timeframe we want to use (daily, hourly, weekly), which asset we want to trade (low spread asset, volatile asset), which market we want to trade (forex, stocks, crypto), do we want to be overnight exposed, etc.,

Figure 17.1: Trading plan component

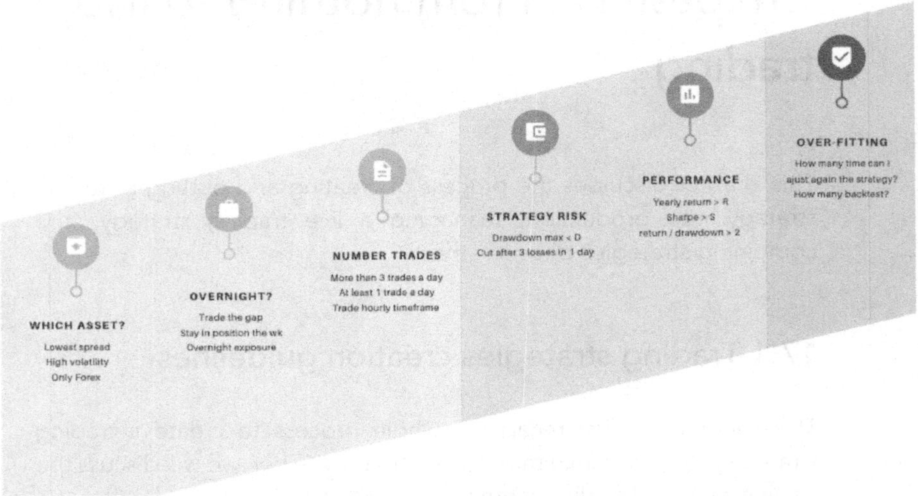

This is an example of the different things we can incorporate into our trading plan; it is not an exhaustive list. Feel free to create your own, according to your attempts.

To conclude, the trading plan will allow us to plan which type of strategy we want to begin the research process peacefully.

> We have to think about all the main characteristics of our strategy before doing the research. It is important not to change the plan because we do not find what we want; keep searching! Find a trading strategy it demands, on average, 100 tries.

17.1.2 The process of a trading strategy building

Creating a trading strategy requires discipline, creativity, and practice. We need to follow several steps:

1. Make **a trading plan** which will accept or reject a strategy. Always create it before doing anything, so we do not have to adjust the attempt in the future if the coding part is too hard.

2. **Importing the data** seems easy, but it is crucial; remember the quote: "garbage in, garbage out." So, be careful of the source we use and always import as much data as possible from the broker.

3. **The preprocessing part** contains the features and target engineering, transformation like standardization, and PCA. It will help the algorithm to understand the relationship between the data better.

4. **Model** the target behavior using machine learning or deep learning algorithms in our case or simple conditions if we use only technical analysis or price action.

5. **Backtest** the strategy two times maximum to avoid overfitting the results and losing our capital in the future.

6. Apply the prediction according to the trading plan during incubation (entry and exit conditions, take-profit, stop-loss)

7. Check the incubation results and compare them to the backtest results to see if the distribution is similar (more details in the following section)

8. Repeat this process for each strategy.

As we can see, the process seems simple, but we have taken the whole book to explain it. So, please do not underestimate the difficulty of this process; we will need at least 100 tries to find one good strategy (on average). Do not give up and be stable in our work; you will find profitable strategies but it requires much time.

17.1.3 Trading journal

In discretionary (manual) trading, the trading journal contains information about each trade you will pass on the market: entry and exit, take-profit, stop-loss, bet sizing, risk management, etc.

The goal is to have a trading journal (the practice) as close as possible to the trading plan (theory). However, when we work on an algorithmic trading project, we will adopt a different approach. Why? Because all the parameters are set using the algo, they cannot change. So, what will we write in our trading journal?

When we work on algorithmic trading, we also need a trading journal, but for several other things:

- Analyze the trade manually and write what you think about it: positive and negative points to correct. Here is an idea to understand the utility better:
  - Stop-loss above the support too many times → Define another way to place stop-loss.
  - False signals after some news → Do not trade 1 hour before some news.
  - Checking about the return's distribution between production and backtest and see that the production returns are less and less → Upgrade the strategy or stop it
- Keep an history of the coding issue and how to solve them; it is valuable when we are on other projects to solve our issues easily.

17.2 Do not put all your eggs in one basket

We thought that once we had a profitable strategy, the work was done. No, once we have one strategy, we need to create others to combine them and find a robust trading strategies portfolio.

17.2.1 Bet sizing

The first rule is that we will NEVER invest all our capital in one strategy. It is simple, but it is essential. Moreover, there are several simple rules to follow to minimize the risk of losing much money:

1. Never risk more than 1% of your capital in one trade (adapt the volume)

2. Depending on strategy, stop the algo for the day after 3 losses or stop it for the week after 5% loss, etc.

If we use compounded interest, let us see the danger of taking too prominent positions. In figure 17.1, we see that the more the position size increases, the more the risk of being a losing trader increases.

Figure 17.1: Chances to be a losing trader depending on the bet size

As we can see, if we have 50% chances to win 1% or 50% chances to lose 1%, with one trade per day over one year, the chances of being a losing trader is around 52%. However, if we increase the bet size from 1% to 30% per trade, we see that the chances of being a losing trader are around 100%. It is logical because after three consecutive losing trades, it left only 10% of our capital, and we will need 900% of earnings to come back to our initial amount.

The main point of bet sizing is that it is better to use compounded interest to obtain the benefit of exponential growth, but we need to manage risk because the more the loss is significant, the more it is not easy to come back to the initial amount as shown in figure 17.2

Figure 17.2: Necessary profit to recover a x% loss

Losse	10%	20%	30%	40%	50%	60%	70%	80%	90%
Necessary profit (simple)	10%	20%	30%	40%	50%	60%	70%	80%	90%
Necessary profit (coumpounded)	11%	25%	43%	66%	100%	150%	233%	400%	900%

As we can see, using compounded interest (represented by a dynamic lot in trading), the more the loss is big, the more it is difficult to return to the initial amount.

17.2.2 Why create a trading strategy portfolio?

There are many reasons to create a trading strategy portfolio. The best way to create it is to check uncorrelated assets or, even better, a negative correlation between assets.

 Above all, creating a trading strategy portfolio is essential to reduce the risk of your investment: drawdown, VaR, etc...

Mainly, suppose we use leverage and compounded interest. In that case, we need to create a portfolio to diversify our risk and decrease the position risk (which is possible by increasing the number of trading strategies). Moreover, the portfolio and the bet sizing parts fit very well together because the more we add trading strategies to the portfolio, the more we can decrease the weight of one strategy in the portfolio and then create a robust investment strategy.

The main point of creating a trading strategy portfolio is to decrease the portfolio's drawdown while keeping a comfortable return. Let us see an example.

Figure 17.3: Portfolio advantage compared to individual strategy

As we see, combining the strategy, the portfolio return is the mean between the three strategies. However, the main point is that the drawdown is very low compared to an individual strategy.

17.3. Live trading process

The live trading process is not the hardest part, but if there is one error in this, we will lose a lot of money. So, we need to be as meticulous as possible.

17.3.1. Safety first

When we put our strategy into live trading, we need to pay attention to the security of our capital. So, the best way to do it is to place some securities like the following example:

1. Stop the algorithm after X% loss in one day: It will be good to do it if the algo does something wrong, like taking 100 positions simultaneously. However, we need to backtest the consecutive losses in one-day distribution to find the best value. For example, suppose we see that there is only a 1% chance of having more than two losing trades a day. In that case, we can put the following security: "if we have three losing trades a day, we stop the algorithm for the day."

2. Stop the algorithm after X% loss in one month: sometimes, the market conditions can be tough for our algorithm; try to find the best moment to stop it in the backtest and check the performance considering that we stop the algorithm in some market situations.

3. Stop the algorithm if the drawdown in live trading becomes two times higher than the drawdown in incubation: it is very interesting to find when an algo needs to be stopped, but we will discuss it later in the chapter.

These three rules are not exhaustive; there are a lot of different similar rules to manage our risk and be a profitable trader.

17.3.2 Incubation phase

This part is one of the most important. In this part, we will check if our theoretical profitable trading strategy can be put into live trading or not. Fortunately, it is the easiest part of the project on the programming side. However, it is the hardest on the psychological side also. So, let us see all the process in detail:

1. We put our strategy in incubation on a demo account or with very small capital in live trading to check how the strategy works in live trading. We need to understand if we have not made any mistakes or forgotten something essential for the profitability of the strategy.

2. WE NEED TO CHOOSE IF WE KEEP THE STRATEGY: it seems easy, but it is not. After one month minimum of live trading, we need to check if the results of the incubation are good or not.

How to tell if the incubation returns are good or not? There are many ways, but here is the easiest one. To do it, we can compare the distribution between the backtest returns and the incubation returns. The best way to do it is to compare the statistics with the theoretical values obtained in the backtest on the train and test sets. Then compute the return in the incubation period using our backtest function.

It will be exciting to understand if we do not make any mistakes because we should have something very close. Let us see the following figure with two cases to understand when we have a problem or not.

Figure 17.4: two situations after an incubation period

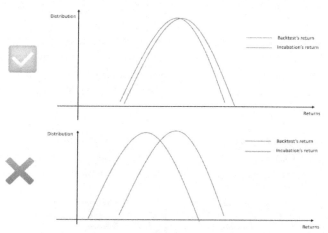

As we can see, the first distributions are similar instead of to the seconds, so we need to review all our code to find the issue (frequent in the backtest function).

> You can use a Kolmogorov statistical test to compare two distributions if you need to automatize the process instead of doing it using graph only.

17.3.3 When to quit?

It is the eternal question of when the algorithm needs to be stopped. It is very difficult to say that, and we need to adapt our analysis to the market conditions. It is a subjective choice.

However, we can find some tips to stop the algo, especially computation about the drawdown: the method is called the drawdown management method.

It is simple to understand that we stop the algorithm when the drawdown falls below a threshold. So, the goal when we have stopped the algorithm is to determine if we will activate the algorithm again or not! To do this, there are no rules. However, we need to analyze the strategy's performance from A to Z. If the performances were extraordinary and during the COVID crisis, we have an abnormal drawdown, and the algorithm shutdown; then, then I personally will put the algo again in production when I see that the market conditions are normal.. In the second case, if we have an algorithm with stable returns and from 6 months ago to now, the drawdown does not stop increasing, , I will not activate it after the drawdown management shutdown.

I hope you have enjoyed the book. Do not hesitate to join the discord forum (QRCODE in chapter 1) if you have questions about the book or see the other traders' questions. I wish you a fantastic continuation!

Annex: Compounding versus simple interest

This paper will learn the difference between the compounding interest strategy and the simple interest strategy. We will explain why the difference between these types of calculations. Then, we will see how to compute the cumulative returns using these methods.

What is the difference between the simple and the compounding methods?

The simple interest strategy is a fixed lot strategy. It means that each day, we will invest capital C. We have a capital C*r. If we simulate this behavior over days, we have the following equation:

$$\pi = C * r_1 + C * r_2 + \cdots + C * r_n$$

$$\pi = C * (r_1 + r_2 + \cdots + r_n)$$

$$\pi = C * \sum_{i=1}^{n} r_i$$

Where π is the strategy's profit, C is the capital invested, and r_i is the return in the percentage of the day i.

However, the compounding interest works with a global multiplicator coefficient. If we have an initial capital of C, the day 1, we have $C *(1 + r_1)$ and day2 $C *(1 + r_1)* (1 + r_2)$. Thus, the day n, we have $C *(1 + r_1) *...* (1 + r_n)$. With this strategy, the whole capital will be invested instead of the simple interest, which constantly invests the same capital:

$$\pi = (C * (1 + r_1) * (1 + r_2) * ... * (1 + r_n)) - 1$$

$$\pi = (\prod_{i=1}^{n} (1 + r_1) * C) - C$$

$$\pi = C * \left(\prod_{i=1}^{n} (1 + r_1) - 1\right)$$

Where π is the strategy's profit, C is the capital invested, and r_i is the return in the percentage of the day i.

How to compute the simple and compounding interest

To compute the cumulative return of a simple interest strategy, we need to compute the cumulative return. To do it, we can use the numpy function cumsum().

Code: Cumulative return using the simple interest method

```
cumulative_return = np.cumsum(returns)
```

However, to compute the cumulative return of a compounding interest strategy, need to use the product of the multiplicator coefficient. To do it, we will use the cumprod() function of numpy.

Code: Cumulative return using the compounding interest method

```
cumulative_return = np.cumprod(1+returns) - 1
```

Annex: Save and load scikit-learn and Tensorflow models

In this paper, we will learn how to save, and load fitted scikit-learn and TensorFlow models. We will begin by saving a scikit-learn model. To do it, we will use the library *pickle* and *joblib* using the following code.

Code: Save and load scikit-learn model

```python
from sklearn.svm import SVC
import pickle
from joblib import dump, load


# Save
svc = SVC()
alg_pickle = pickle.dumps(svc)
dump(alg_pickle, "svc.joblib")


# Load
alg = load("voting.jolib")
```

To save models with TensorFlow, we need to use the command of TensorFlow.

Code: How to save and load TensorFlow models

```python
def create_model():
  # INTIALIZATION SEQUENTIAL MODEL
  classifier = Sequential()


  # AJOUT COUCHE DENSE ET DROPOUT
  for _ in range(nb_hidden_layer):
    classifier.add(Dense(75, input_shape = (X_train.shape[1],),
activation="relu"))


  # AJOUT COUCHE DENSE
  classifier.add(Dense(1, activation="sigmoid"))
```

```python
# COMPILATION DU MODÈLE
classifier.compile(loss="binary_crossentropy", optimizer="adam")


return classifier



# Save the weights
classifier.save_weights('classifier')


# Create a new model instance
model = create_model()


# Restore the weights
model.load_weights('classifier')
```

Annex: MetaTrader class

For more information about the configuration of MetaTrader device.
Check the README.md file of the Github repository (link available in
chapter 1).

```python
import warnings
from datetime import datetime
import pandas as pd
import MetaTrader5 as mt5
warnings.filterwarnings("ignore")
mt5.initialize()



class MT5:

    def get_data(symbol, n, timeframe=mt5.TIMEFRAME_D1):
        """ Function to import the data of the chosen symbol"""

        # Initialize the connection if there is not
        mt5.initialize()

        # Current date extract
        utc_from = datetime.now()

        # Import the data into a tuple
        rates = mt5.copy_rates_from(symbol, timeframe, utc_from, n)

        # Tuple to dataframe
        rates_frame = pd.DataFrame(rates)

        # Convert time in seconds into the datetime format
        rates_frame['time']    =    pd.to_datetime(rates_frame['time'],
unit='s')

        # Convert the column "time" in the right format
        rates_frame['time']    =    pd.to_datetime(rates_frame['time'],
format='%Y-%m-%d')
```

```python
        # Set column time as the index of the dataframe
        rates_frame = rates_frame.set_index('time')
        return rates_frame


    def orders(symbol, lot, buy=True, id_position=None):
        """ Send the orders """

        # Initialize the connection if there is not
        if mt5.initialize() == False:
            mt5.initialize()


        # Filling order mode (you need to try 0,1 or 2
        # because it is depending of the broker)
        i = 1


        # Take ask price
        ask_price = mt5.symbol_info_tick(symbol).ask


        # Take bid price
        bid_price = mt5.symbol_info_tick(symbol).bid


        # Take the point of the asset
        point = mt5.symbol_info(symbol).point


        deviation = 20   # mt5.getSlippage(symbol)
        #*********************** Open a trade *************************
        if id_position == None:

            # Buy order Parameters
            if buy:
                type_trade = mt5.ORDER_TYPE_BUY
                sl = ask_price - 100 * point
                tp = ask_price + 100 * point
                price = ask_price

            # Sell order Parameters
            else:
```

```python
            type_trade = mt5.ORDER_TYPE_SELL
            sl = bid_price + 100 * point
            tp = bid_price - 100 * point
            price = bid_price


        # Open the trade
        request = {
            "action": mt5.TRADE_ACTION_DEAL,
            "symbol": symbol,
            "volume": lot,
            "type": type_trade,
            "price": price,
            "deviation": deviation,
            "sl": sl,
            "tp": tp,
            "magic": 234000,
            "comment": "python script order",
            "type_time": mt5.ORDER_TIME_GTC,
            "type_filling": i,
        }
        # send a trading request
        result = mt5.order_send(request)
        result_comment = result.comment


    # *************************** Close a trade ***********************
    else:
        # Buy order Parameters
        if buy:
            type_trade = mt5.ORDER_TYPE_SELL
            price = bid_price


        # Sell order Parameters
        else:
            type_trade = mt5.ORDER_TYPE_BUY
            price = ask_price


        # Close the trade
        request = {
```

```python
        "action": mt5.TRADE_ACTION_DEAL,

        "symbol": symbol,

        "volume": lot,

        "type": type_trade,

        "position": id_position,

        "price": price,

        "deviation": deviation,

        "magic": 234000,

        "comment": "python script order",

        "type_time": mt5.ORDER_TIME_GTC,

        "type_filling": i,

    }


    # send a trading request
    result = mt5.order_send(request)
    result_comment = result.comment
    return result.comment


def resume():
    """ Return the current positions. Position=0 --> Buy """
    # Initialize the connection if there is not
    mt5.initialize()


    # Define the name of the columns that we will create
    colonnes = ["ticket", "position", "symbol", "volume"]


    # Go take the current open trades
    current = mt5.positions_get()


    # Create a empty dataframe
    summary = pd.DataFrame()


    # Loop to add each row in dataframe
    # (Can be ameliorate using of list of list)
    for element in current:
        element_pandas = pd.DataFrame([element.ticket,
                                       element.type,
                                       element.symbol,
```

```python
                                        element.volume],
                                    index=colonnes).transpose()
        summary = pd.concat((summary, element_pandas), axis=0)


    return summary



def run(symbol, long, short, lot):

    # Initialize the connection if there is not
    if mt5.initialize() == False:
        mt5.initialize()

    # Choose your  symbol
    print("-----------------------------------------------------------")
    print("Date: ", datetime.now().strftime("%Y-%m-%d %H:%M:%S"))
    print("SYMBOL:", symbol)

    # Initialize the device
    current_open_positions = MT5.resume()
    # Buy or sell
    print(f"BUY: {long} \t  SHORT: {short}")

    """ Close trade eventually """
    # Extraction type trade
    try:
        position                                                     =
current_open_positions.loc[current_open_positions["symbol"]==symbol].val
ues[0][1]

        identifier                                                   =
current_open_positions.loc[current_open_positions["symbol"]==symbol].val
ues[0][0]
    except:
        position= None
        identifier = None

    print(f"POSITION: {position} \t ID: {identifier}")
```

```python
        # Close trades
        if long==True and position==0:
            long=False


        elif long==False and position==0:
            res = MT5.orders(symbol, lot, buy=True, id_position=
identifier)
            print(f"CLOSE LONG TRADE: {res}")


        elif short==True and position ==1:
            short=False


        elif short == False and position == 1:
            res = MT5.orders(symbol, lot, buy=False, id_position=
identifier)
            print(f"CLOSE SHORT TRADE: {res}")


        else:
            pass



        """ Buy or short """
        if long==True:


            res = MT5.orders(symbol, lot, buy=True, id_position=None)
            print(f"OPEN LONG TRADE: {res}")


        if short==True:
            res = MT5.orders(symbol, lot, buy=False, id_position=None)
            print(f"OPEN SHORT TRADE: {res}")


        print("-------------------------------------------------------")

    def close_all_night():
        result = MT5.resume()
        for i in range(len(result)):
            before = mt5.account_info().balance
```

```python
        row = result.iloc[0+i:1+i,:]
        if row["position"][0]==0:
            res  =  MT5.orders(row["symbol"][0],  row["volume"][0],
buy=True, id_position=row["ticket"][0])

        else:
            res  =  MT5.orders(row["symbol"][0],  row["volume"][0],
buy=False, id_position=row["ticket"][0])
```

Additional readings

Chapter 3

- Markowitz's "Portfolio Selection ": A Fifty-Year Retrospective, The University of Chicago Press
  https://www.jstor.org/stable/269777
- Portfolio management: mean-variance analysis in the US asset market, Narela (Bajram) Spaseski,
  https://www.researchgate.net/publication/264423979_PORT FOLIO_MANAGEMENT_MEAN-VARIANCE_ANALYSIS_IN_THE_US_ASSET_MARKET
- Mean-variance-skewness-kurtosis based portfolio optimization, KingKeung Lai, Shouyang Wand, Lean yu
  https://citeseerx.ist.psu.edu/viewdoc/download?doi=10.1.1.898.991&rep=rep1&type=pdf

Chapter 4

- Tactical Asset Allocation (TAA), ADAM BARONE.
  https://www.investopedia.com/terms/t/tacticalassetallocation.asp

Chapter 5

- Optimization of conditional value-at-risk, R. Tyrrell Rockafellar.
  https://www.ise.ufl.edu/uryasev/files/2011/11/CVaR1_JOR.pdf

Chapter 7

- Stationarity and differencing.
  https://people.duke.edu/~rnau/411diff.htm
- Cointegration, Niti Gupta.
  https://www.wallstreetmojo.com/cointegration/
- Pairs Trading, James Chen.
  https://www.investopedia.com/terms/p/pairstrade.asp

Chapter 8

- What Is a Time Series?, Adam Hayes.
  https://www.investopedia.com/terms/t/timeseries.asp

- Autoregressive–moving-average model, Wikipedia. https://en.wikipedia.org/wiki/Autoregressive–moving-average_model

Chapter 9
- Linear Regression for Machine Learning, Jason Brownlee. https://machinelearningmastery.com/linear-regression-for-machine-learning/

Chapter 11
- Support-vector machine, Wikipedia. https://en.wikipedia.org/wiki/Support-vector_machine

Chapter 12
- Decision Trees in Machine Learning, Prashant Gupta. https://towardsdatascience.com/decision-trees-in-machine-learning-641b9c4e8052
- Ensemble Methods in Machine Learning: What are They and Why Use Them? Evan Lutins. https://towardsdatascience.com/ensemble-methods-in-machine-learning-what-are-they-and-why-use-them-68ec3f9fef5f

Chapter 13
- Stochastic Gradient Descent — Clearly Explained !!, Aishwarya V Srinivasan. https://towardsdatascience.com/stochastic-gradient-descent-clearly-explained-53d239905d31

Chapter 14
- Recurrent Neural Networks cheatsheet, Afshine Amidi and Shervine Amidi. https://stanford.edu/~shervine/teaching/cs-230/cheatsheet-recurrent-neural-networks

Chapter 15
- Introduction to Convolutional Neural Networks (CNN), Manav Mandal. https://www.analyticsvidhya.com/blog/2021/05/convolutional-neural-networks-cnn/